REDEMPTION

THE CHURCH IN ANCIENT TIMES

LUKE H. DAVIS

CF4•K

10 9 8 7 6 5 4 3 2

Reprinted in 2024
Paperback ISBN: 978-1-5271-0800-4
Ebook ISBN: 978-1-5271-0884-4

Published by Christian Focus Publications,
Geanies House, Fearn, Tain, Ross-shire,
IV20 1TW, Scotland, U.K.
www.christianfocus.com;
email: info@christianfocus.com

Design and illustration: Laura K. Sayers
Cover design: James Amour

Printed and bound in Malaysia

Luke Davis has written a very accessible and enjoyable introduction to early church history. Based around some of its leading characters, here we can see the early Christian centuries with a human face. An ideal starting point for anyone's first plunge into those formative years of the church's life, faith, and worship.

Dr Nick Needham
Highland Theological College

Redemption: The Church in Ancient Times, part of the Risen Hope series, by Luke Davis, is a fascinating peek into the lives of our early church fathers. His telling of their stories brings the reader to key historical moments in church history. He puts flesh on them in such a way that we can understand the controversies and persecutions they battled both inside and outside of the church, see their humanity, frail and faltering at times, yet visibly strengthened by the Holy Spirit for the specific season in the life of the church. This very readable church history series will strengthen the faith of young and old alike. A perfect family read aloud, or companion to world history studies for homeschoolers or Christian school students, or those who would like an initial foray into the often confusing and overwhelming realm of church history. This series makes it clear, enjoyably so.

Cathleen Smythe, Middle School teacher,
former homeschooler, Children's Ministry Director
(Truth Point Church)

Redemption: The Church in Ancient Times: Engaging, captivating and informative! Redemption; The Church in Ancient Times by Luke Davis takes you on a journey with the Early Church. Whilst astounding you with interesting historic facts and dates, Luke manages to revive stories so it actually feels like you're walking and talking with the people at the time. This book is exciting, it is dramatic, it will capture your imagination and it will inform your mind about what God did through the Early Church.

Alistair Chalmers,
Assistant Pastor of Bruntsfield Evangelical Church, Edinburgh

Once a man lived and died in poverty, unaware of the buried treasure beneath his property. Even so, the Christian church today is at risk of forgetting the riches of its own history. It matters little how magnificent the stories may be, if the truth remains buried, or if the records are locked away in archaic or arcane language that people cannot grasp. In *Redemption* and *Reign*, Luke Davis selects pivotal moments from history, to which he applies an imagination like that of a Hollywood filmmaker. The past jumps into razor-sharp focus, as the reader sees, hears, and feels these episodes happening once again. Davis is no narrow sectarian, seeking to exalt some believers at the expense of others, but instead approaches the Christian past with generous orthodoxy, finding lessons to be learned in far-flung times and places. These volumes are an ideal first book for younger readers, and—quite frankly—for some not-so-younger readers too. Whatever a reader's age, Davis's books are a perfect appetizer for those tasting the delights of church history for the first time, who will then be likely to return for a full meal.

Michael J. McClymond, Ph.D.
Professor of Modern Christianity
Department of Theological Studies, Saint Louis University
St. Louis, Missouri, USA.

Luke Davis has done an impressive job of telling the history of medieval Christianity for young adults through a skilful use of story and traditional narrative. He has taken seriously the importance of the thousand years of the Middle Ages that many Evangelicals wrongly write off as a spiritual wasteland. This is a period of time when God was at work, when the church got some things right but also made some big mistakes. The entire era has much to teach us. Highly recommended!

Michael A.G. Haykin, The Southern Baptist Theological
Seminary, Louisville, Kentucky

According to the Psalms, God's people praise and glorify Him as they tell of His mighty acts from one generation to the next (Psalm 145:4). Today the church is in need of storytellers who will teach the next generation the great things God has done through His people throughout the centuries. With sparkling prose, backed by solid research, Luke Davis makes church history come alive for the young reader (and readers of all ages!). What makes this work unique is that it offers engaging historical fiction but also provides timelines, factual summaries of significant figures and events, and insightful reflection. This is a powerful combination. You will be inspired to serve the Lord today, as you read of the trials and triumphs of the saints who have gone before us. I look forward to sharing these stories with my children!

Ben Wagner,
Rector, Anglican Church of the Resurrection,
Chesterfield, Missouri

CONTENTS

DEDICATED TO

Rev. Tony Giles

wise guide,
marvelous mentor,
dear friend

with highest honor and deepest thanks

IMPORTANT MOMENTS IN THE ANCIENT CHURCH

3-4 BC
Jesus Christ is born in Bethlehem

AD 28-29
Death, resurrection, and ascension of Jesus

29
Pentecost; Peter's sermon; 3000 baptized in one day

47-48
Paul's first missionary journey

64-67
Great Fire of Rome; Peter, Paul are martyred

70
Destruction of Jerusalem

81-96
Persecution of the Church under Domitian

98
Death of John; end of apostolic age

110
Ignatius martyred at Rome

155
Polycarp martyred in Smyrna

165

Justin martyred

177

Irenaeus, student of Polycarp, named bishop of Lyons

205

Origen begins teaching in Alexandria

250-260

Persecution under Decian and Valerian

258

Cyprian martyred in Carthage

284

Intense persecution under Diocletian begins

312

Constantine's victory at the Milvian Bridge

313

Edict of Milan

315

Arian controversy erupts in Alexandria

325

Council of Nicea affirms Jesus as the eternal Son of God

328

Athanasius named bishop of Alexandria

381
Council of Constantinople affirms deity of Holy Spirit

386
Ambrose bars Arians from worship in Milan

398
John Chrysostom named bishop of Constantinople

400
Augustine completes his Confessions

405
Jerome publishes the full Vulgate Bible in Latin

410
Visigoth king Alaric conquers Rome

413
Augustine begins writing The City of God

431
Council of Ephesus condemns Nestorianism

432
Patrick undertakes his mission to Ireland

451
Council of Chalcedon declares Christ fully divine and fully human

476
Roman Empire defeated by the Germans under Odoacer

THE ANCIENT CHURCH

At no point were the hopes of the Christian faith more frayed than when Jesus ascended into heaven in Acts 1. After three years of ministry with twelve disciples by His side, Jesus had left them to continue His work. While Jesus was on earth, His disciples struggled to understand His teaching, assumed His kingship meant something totally different than what Jesus intended, and ran away from Him when He was captured and led to death. And Jesus was putting the responsibility for guiding the Church into their hands? Surely a disaster in the waiting?

Yet that was hardly what happened. The Holy Spirit's influence upon the disciples made them bold ambassadors for the good news of Jesus' saving death and resurrection. Against much resistance, the Gospel (the term Christians have given to this "good news") spread throughout the Roman Empire. The disciples—who became known as apostles—were sent out, along with a new ally named Paul, to start new churches in cities within and beyond Israel. The message of Christ swept through Caesarea, Antioch, northwest into Asia Minor, and across into Greece and onward to Rome and beyond.

All this took place despite much persecution against Christians. Some Roman emperors were more direct in their policies of resistance, some preferred to let local leaders manage a response to the growing Church. Yet, Christians had to be watchful. They knew of the promise of Jesus, that as the world had hated Him, the world would hate them, as well. In some cases, the persecution was so intense that a number of Christians were martyred—

killed because of their unwavering faith. Bishops such as Ignatius, Polycarp, and Cyprian were among them, and the list of other Christ-followers who lost their lives could fill many books.

Despite persecution, the Church throughout the world continued to grow, attracting new followers with its message of the grace of God through Jesus Christ. The Christian faith was shown in a lifestyle that honored the human family, dignified women, sought out abandoned babies and children to give them loving homes, and recognized the inherent worth of people in the lowest parts of society. All this happened even though the Church was looked down upon by the ruling class, and the Christian faith was increasingly marginalized.

All this changed with the ascension of Constantine as undisputed emperor. Due to a visionary experience before a key battle, Constantine believed the God of the Christians had given him the victory that sealed his kingly power. In response, Constantine authorized full freedom of worship for the Church and gave high honor to Christians. Overnight, followers of Jesus went from being hunted targets to esteemed citizens. The liberty they now enjoyed could set them more at ease. It could also create some tensions that had not been there before.

In time, various teachings about Jesus caused confusion and competition within the larger Church. Arius and Athanasius would engage in a verbal battle over the nature of Jesus. Was He the eternal Son of God, or was He the first and most worthy created being? Constantine—not wanting his newly-won empire to fall into disorder—commanded that these tensions be settled in a council of bishops at Nicea. There, the Nicene Creed demonstrated the biblical truth that Jesus was the eternal Son of God, but for years afterward, arguments continued to rage. Many other councils followed to deal with other questions. "How is Jesus both God and human?" "How are we saved from sin?" It seemed the more freedom the Church enjoyed; the more questions rose from within demanding answers.

This is not to say that Christians were left ignorant in their search for truth. The Church produced many great writers, thinkers, bishops, and pastors to offer deep and practical guidance. Justin Martyr, Tertullian, Origen, Athanasius, Ambrose, John Chrysostom, Jerome, and Augustine explained and clarified Scriptural teaching. Gregory the Illuminator boldly returned to his homeland of Armenia determined to preach Christ to his people, and the former slave Patrick courageously took the Christian faith that had settled in Britain and went to Ireland to convert a pagan land.

The story of the ancient Church is one of a people who were finding their way over many years by God's light. We must recognize that the beginnings of this movement were difficult, and these followers of Jesus struggled at times to speak to the world around them. Today, we are looking back over the centuries with many more years of understanding. If anything, we should be able to empathize with our fellow believers in ages past, for we stand on the shoulders of those who braved persecution, death, debate, and mystery on behalf of generations to come.

ROME
WICKLOW
PHILIPPI
CONSTANTINOPLE
SMYRNA
CARTHAGE
BETHLEHEM

PETER

Pentecost in Jerusalem, A.D. 28 or 29

Peter took the leftover bread from the low table, tearing it in half and wincing as he did so. *I wouldn't think that remaining inside rather than fishing on the sea would exhaust me so much,* he thought. Although he had a similar pallet bed at home in Galilee, sleeping in a different location meant fitful nights and less rest. Being away from the sea also affected his joints and muscles. His fingers ached; his back cried out for relief, and every time he ascended and descended the steps in this house, his ankles crackled like a Roman chariot over loose stones. He chewed the bread and looked up as Matthias entered the upper room.

"A blessed morning, Peter," Matthias spoke cheerily, his voice fully confident yet without a trace of bombast. The apostles had just selected Matthias to join their company the day before, but rather than being puffed up with pride, the newly minted apostle seemed eager to learn and follow.

"Good morning, Matthias," Peter replied, pressing his left palm down to the floor and pushing himself gingerly into a standing position. "I assume all are gathered downstairs?"

"They are," Matthias responded, "and several of the women just got here. Salome and Joanna had taken bread to the Temple so they would be among the early crowd. But all the brothers are downstairs, with Mary and Mary Magdalene."

All in perfect harmony?" Peter chuckled, knowing Matthias would understand his gentle sarcasm.

"We might be by the end of the day, Peter," he said, "but if anyone can quell their disagreements, you can."

Peter shook his head as he moved toward the door. "Matthias, if you knew me over the last three years, you'd know what a dangerous idea that is."

"I don't know Him!"

"I've never met the man!"

"Curse you, I don't even know this Jesus you're talking about!"

The words remained imprinted in his soul. No amount of pain in his weary body could compare with the anguish of knowing that he had denied Jesus on the eve of the Master's death! He remembered the crowing of the rooster; he recalled the pained look in Jesus' eyes.

And yet the day came, after Jesus had miraculously risen from death, that they met by the Sea of Galilee. While the others cooked a morning breakfast of fresh fish, Jesus had pulled Peter aside.

"Simon, son of John, do you love me?" the Lord asked him.

"Yes, Lord," Peter said, remembering how Jesus would call him by his original name. "You know that I love you."

"Then I ask you to feed my lambs.""I will, Jesus."

A painful pause, then Jesus said, "Simon, son of John, do you love me?"

"Jesus, you know I do. Of course, the answer is yes!"

"Then, tend my sheep."

The pause. How painful. But Peter knew what was coming.

"Peter, do you love me?"

Jesus had asked again. Three times Peter had denied Him. Three times his Master pursued him. And that's when Peter understood. *This is grace. This is grace.*

"You know everything, Lord. I love you, always and forever."

"Then feed my sheep. Truly, truly, I say to you, when you were young, you used to dress yourself and walk wherever you wanted, but when you are old, you will stretch out your hands, and another will dress you and carry you where you do not want to go."

Why do you continue to pursue me, Lord? Peter wondered. But he felt his Master's hand on his shoulder.

"I cannot imagine why you have called me, Jesus," Peter whispered, barely able to fathom the words of his Lord, "but you have said it will be so, and so I accept."

"Peter! Peter!"

Matthias' words pierced his trance. Looking around the room, he saw them all. Men who had been with him over the last three years, through hope and anguish. The women who had assisted and encouraged them. Jesus' mother, Mary, with the other ladies. Other men who simply desired to come and pray, for they had no other place to go.

"We are all here?" he asked.

His brother Andrew nodded. "We are waiting for you to speak, Peter. We have selected Matthias to join us. We have prayed for several days. What is the next step?"

"To do what we have been doing," Peter said firmly. "We must pray."

"Pray?" The question, posed sharply, came from Bartholomew. "I appreciate your desire to seek guidance from God, Peter, but how long will this go on? Do you not remember what Jesus told us before he was lifted into heaven? 'Go therefore, and make disciples of all nations'! How are we to make more disciples if we as disciples remain here? How are we to baptize others if we never leave this house?"

"Agreed!" called out Simon.

John rolled his eyes. "Oh, not you! Spoken like a true Zealot! Unless we're on the move uprooting everything, we're not making progress!"

"Have a care, John," Peter whispered, gesturing him to be quiet. "He's just expressing his opinion."

"We've had our time for prayer," Simon continued, "and now it's time for action!"

"It is time to listen, Simon," Matthew spoke up, "and if we would stop making our own plans, maybe we will discover God's!"

"All right," Peter raised his voice a touch above the others, "let's just consider this. We are putting out a lot of our own words. Maybe we should remember Jesus' words? Yes, Bartholomew, he said to go, to make disciples, and to baptize. But he didn't say when! The pace at which we travel must join with Jesus' pace, not the other way around. But he definitely said to wait here in Jerusalem for what the Father has promised, to be baptized with the Holy Spirit. If we wish to receive that promise, we should wish to obey our Lord. Jesus never told us how long to wait; he only told us what to do. Obedience and prayer is the order of the day."

James shifted in the corner of the room. "I am in full agreement with you, Peter, no matter what danger might come our way. Because I realize if I proclaim Jesus, that is a costly enterprise that could cost me my life. But you do also understand, Peter, that this task seems very overwhelming."

"What do you mean?" asked Andrew.

"What James is saying," said Thaddeus, "is to think about our time with Jesus, all of us. Think about all he said and did that we didn't understand at the time, how clouded in mind and heart we could be. We weren't exactly shining examples of spiritual hope when Jesus was still here. And now he's gone, and he wants us to carry on His work! We were bumblers when Jesus lived among us. What about now?"

Peter put his hands up for quiet. "I can appreciate all of this, Thaddeus. I really can. There are over ten dozen of us crowded in this house today. I know you all, and you know me. You all know that I denied Jesus the night before His death. James and John can tell stories about their pride. Judas betrayed our Lord, which is why we've had Matthias join us. And even when Jesus gathered us all together on that day he departed into heaven, some of you expressed your doubts that he had really risen from the dead. I agree it seems pretty poor strategy to entrust Jesus' plan with us, except for one thing." He paused before going on. "Jesus said to us, 'You will receive power when the Holy Spirit has come upon you, and you will be my witnesses in Jerusalem and in all Judea and Samaria, and to the end of the earth.'" I do not know how that will happen, brothers and sisters, but I know Jesus has promised to make it happen. And if he says we should keep praying until we receive that, so be it."

A murmur went through the group. Even Simon, the political firebrand, softened his eyes and nodded his head. One by one, they closed their eyes and bowed their heads. And prayed.

Peter did not know how long they had been praying. It was an unusually cool and somewhat overcast day, but from the position of the sun, it could not have been past the third hour. He thought little of the sound of the wind, and joining hands with Mary and Philip, he went back to praying when he opened one eye and looked out the window.

Strange, he thought, I hear the sound of a stiff gale from the sea, and yet no trees outside are moving.

And then, it happened! A furious blast shot through the whole of the room, lifting Thomas out of his kneeling position and knocking Peter over! The women clutched each other.

"Brother, what's going on?" Andrew pleaded.

Peter's body aches surged into abject pain. "I don't know, Andrew. This is worse than any storm we had when fishing, but..."

Amongst the cries and calls of the throng, Peter never got to complete his sentence. The wind howled once more, cascading in form into rippling, concentric circles above their heads!

"Peter!" cried John. "What is this?"

"Maybe," Peter croaked, "this is the end of our waiting."

And with that, the ripples of the gale collapsed with a loud crack, and the room was filled with a blinding light. Peter shielded his eyes as he scrambled to his feet, reaching down to steady himself on one of the other disciples. It happened to be his brother, Andrew, who looked up at him.

"Brother," Andrew panted, "what is that on your head?"

"I was about to ask you the same question about yourself," Peter coughed.

When the wind had ceased Peter saw the others within the room scrambling to their feet. His brother: James. John. Philip. Thomas. All the disciples, including Matthias. And there it was, hovering over each of their heads.

Fire.

And there it was, burning within his heart.

The promise! He thought. We've received the promised Spirit!

And then he recalled Jesus' words...You shall be my witnesses.

It didn't surprise Peter that they all moved toward the door at once, and moments later they were spilling into the streets of Jerusalem.

The response was overwhelming, and Peter could not have scripted the story any better. Andrew was preaching about the death and resurrection of Jesus, with a throng of devout Jews from Carthage and Cyrene, and from the looks on their faces they understood every word! A crowd of Jews from Antioch latched on to Bartholomew. At the same time Philip was speaking to several families from Iconium in Asia. Even Simon was happily telling of Jesus to a cluster of Parthians obviously far from home. All over the streets a wild conversation had sprung up, and Peter and the others found all enthralled by what they had to say. And all around them they heard the questions spring up.

"What is going on?"

"I know of these folks. Aren't they from Galilee in the north?"

"If that's so, how are they speaking our language?"

"This is outrageous!"

"This is amazing!"

"What does it mean?"

Finally, Peter saw one of them striding toward him as he spoke of Jesus rising from the dead to a group of children from Caesarea. "Oh, God be with me now. It's the son of the high priest."

"You there!" The accuser spat. "What do you mean by disturbing a peaceful Shavuot morning? Are you drunk? That's what this is!" He spread his arms wide, gesturing to the crowd, others calling out agreement. "They're filled with too much new wine, the drunkards!"

Peter, excusing himself from the children, rushed into the crowd's midst.

"Men of Judea," he called out, "and all who dwell this day in Jerusalem, listen to what I have to say. Use reason! How could we be drunk? It's only nine o'clock in the morning! Rather than assuming the worst, perhaps it is wise to believe this is a fulfillment of a promise long ago!"

"A promise?" shouted a farmer from Derbe.

"From the prophet Joel, where he said of old, 'And it shall come to pass afterward, that I will pour out my Spirit on all flesh; your sons and your daughters shall prophesy, your old men shall dream dreams, and your young men shall see visions. Even on the male and female servants in those days I will pour out my Spirit. And I will show wonders in the heavens and on the earth, blood and fire and columns of smoke. The sun shall be turned to darkness, and the moon to blood, before the great and awesome day of the Lord comes. And it shall come to pass that everyone who calls on the name of the Lord shall be saved.'"

The assembly had hushed. Peter looked over at Andrew, James, and John. Their eyes widened, they nodded to him to proceed.

"Men of Israel," he continued, "hear what I say: Jesus of Nazareth, a man proven by God to you through public wonders and miracles—this Jesus, the one given over by God in His sovereign plan, the one whom you crucified, our God raised Him up, shattering death which was powerless to hold our Lord Jesus Christ!"

The crowd gasped, overwhelmed by the news. Peter went on for several minutes as they began to tremble and weep at the words of Jesus' death and resurrection!

"We are all witnesses of these things, you see," he continued, "that Jesus is raised and exalted at God's right hand, and now in this day our Jesus has richly poured out the Holy Spirit upon us, as you can clearly see! So, know with certainty that God has made this Jesus, whom you put to death, both Lord and God!"

Whatever the people had seen and heard that day, nothing compared to the power they felt from Peter's words. A woman clutched at the feet of John and wept. Several rushed to the place where Peter stood, asking, "Brothers, what should we do?"

Peter raised his hands for quiet, then spoke firmly yet with deep passion: "Repent and be baptized, every one of you, in the name of Jesus Christ for the forgiveness of your sins, and you will receive the gift of the Holy Spirit! For this is a promise, a promise for you and for your children and for those in the most distant coastlands: everyone whom the Lord our God calls to himself! Come and be saved!"

A multitude of people swarmed forward, tears coursing doing their cheeks and prayers of repentance spilling from their lips. Calls for water for baptism went up, and in the swarm, Peter and the apostles led them toward a nearby pool. He felt a tap on his shoulder. It was Matthias.

"Did you see, Peter?"

"See what?"

Matthias pointed to the sky. "You speak of Jesus, and the sun breaks out overhead! I don't think that was a coincidence."

Peter smiled, keeping pace with the crowd moving briskly toward the pool. He couldn't believe it. There must be about three thousand people here!

Yes, the promise of the Lord was sure.

"Peter, do you love me? Feed my sheep."

The story of **PETER** is one of dramatic grace. During Jesus' ministry, Peter was known for speaking truth boldly but also for being too rash and overconfident. Yet, Jesus was determined to take who Peter was and work within him for moments such as this. The Pentecost sermon was an event instrumental in bringing many into the church at Jerusalem. For many years, Peter would serve as an apostle, sent to proclaim salvation found in Jesus Christ, and he had a special heart for Jewish believers who became Christians. His travels ranged from Judea all the way to Rome, where it is likely he met his death as a martyr.

BYZANTIUM
BLACK SEA
ASIA
EPHESUS
GALATIA
COLOSSAE
LYSTRA
CAPPADOCIA
TARSUS
EDESSA
ANTIOCH
CYPRUS
SYRIA
TRIPOLI
DAMASCUS
ALEXANDRIA
JERICHO
JERUSALEM
JUDEA
EUPHRATES RIVER

PAUL

Philippi in Macedonia, A.D. 49

"This way!" shouted the soldier, his rough fingers digging into Paul's left arm with such strength that Paul lost all sensation between his shoulder and elbow. Gesturing to his fellow guardsman, the soldier signaled toward the city jail and barked at both Paul and Silas, who was firmly in the grip of the other guard. "We have nothing against your religion, but in a Roman city like ours, you were better off saying nothing about your lunacy!"

"I find it interesting that you charge us with lunacy," Paul began, "when all I did was command that evil spirit to come out of the young girl."

Silas was about to say something when Paul silenced him with a quick wide-eyed stare. Looking beyond his friend, Paul saw Luke and Timothy on the edge of the crowd. Almost imperceptibly, Paul shook his head back and forth to their companions. Not now, he thought, just stay safe and we will see you when we can.

"Mind how you go, orator!" the guard sneered as Paul clattered down the steps and away from the pungent smells of the city market. The scents of fish, spices, and rich meats gave way to an overpowering odor of sludge, oil, and standing water. The guard swung an iron door wide open and shoved Paul roughly into the dark and damp. Paul rubbed his arm, desperately trying to bring the feeling back to his muscles as Silas plowed into him from behind.

"Who do you have for me this time, Antonius?" came a voice out of the gloom? A stocky jailer, sword sheathed, straightened up from attending to another prisoner. Paul looked around the circular holding cell. He counted nine other prisoners.

"Troublemakers, Ontarius!" came the guard's reply. "This bald one and his bearded companion here turned the market road into a cauldron of disorder! They decided that calling out against our Roman gods was preferable to passing quietly through. Several men brought them up on these charges and we beat them accordingly. Perhaps a night in the stocks will quiet them before they meet the magistrates tomorrow for judgment!"

"Proclaiming the name and power of Jesus is what we did, good sir," Paul interrupted calmly but firmly. "And perhaps if you had listened to all the evidence, you would have entertained Atalante's words."

"The slave girl who babbles fortunes?" scoffed the second guard. "We are admitting the thoughts of a crazy girl as a measure of reason?"

"Only that she proved what we did," Silas replied.

"My friend Silas is correct," Paul continued, "for she followed us and cried out 'These men are servants of the Most High God, who proclaim to you the way of salvation!' None of this is new. She's been doing this for days while we have traveled to the river banks for prayer with others. All I did was show compassion to someone who was being exploited by others."

The jailer shook his head. "People have to make a living."

Paul fixed him with a level stare. "Then our accusers can do so in more honorable ways than that. Atalante was vexed by an evil spirit, which caused her to speak fortunes, lining her owners' pockets but bringing her nothing. I merely turned to her and said, 'I command you in the name of Jesus Christ to come out of her!'"

"And?" Ontarius asked.

"That's immaterial," Antonius sneered.

"Not so," Paul interjected, "for she quieted herself and now is in her right mind, praising the God of Abraham, Isaac, and Jacob who sent His Son, Jesus, to bring salvation to His people. Her masters knew their money-tin would run empty, so they grabbed us and dragged us before the magistrates."

"There was no disorder?" Ontarius inquired.

"There was when we arrived!" said Antonius.

"Only because those two men stirred the crowd into a frenzy," Silas growled, "telling all who would listen that we were Jews intent on disturbing this city..."

"And," Paul added, "advocating unlawful Roman customs that can neither be accepted nor practiced." He paused, smiling ruefully. "They failed to say what we had actually done. And so that brings us here."

"Not to mention," Silas continued, "that they went ahead and beat us black and blue, without right, given that..."

"Silas!" Paul turned and held out a hand to stay his friend's frustration. "Do not continue. We'll cross that road when we come to it. Let us suffer gladly for the sake of our Master." He held out his hands to Ontarius, who looked past him to the guards.

"Keep them safely," Antonius grumbled. "Under official orders, they are to be bound in stocks. Tomorrow morning, we'll be back to escort them to the council house for their trial." And with that, the guards stormed out.

Paul and Silas watched them go. "Well, Silas," Paul said with a smile. "let's be thankful. We at least have a roof over our heads while we sleep tonight," Paul turned to Ontarius. "And where would you like us to stay?"

Baffled by Paul's cheerfulness, Ontarius gestured toward a nook behind the wall of the cell. "This way, sir, although I can only promise you a solid roof but little comfort."

"My back," Silas groaned. "I am going out of my mind in these stocks."

"They certainly make it difficult to sleep," Paul admitted, turning his head either way to crack his neck for some relief. "However, we should have joy in the promises of Christ."

"Paul, we should have been going to the river to pray with Lydia and the others. We were doing so well. The Lord opened Lydia's heart to receive Jesus Christ, we've baptized so many new believers, and yet now we have run aground in this tomb of a prison."

Paul closed his eyes and prayed, "Lord help me to trust in you. Help me to help Silas to trust in you."

In truth, he could understand his friend's anxiety. They had begun this venture when Paul and his friend Barnabas could not agree on taking young Mark along on another journey. They had finally decided to split up, with Barnabas taking Mark and Paul asking Silas to come through Asia Minor. The pain of that dispute weighed heavily upon Paul at first, although now he saw what God was doing: helping Paul and Barnabas cover twice as much territory apart than together. And then just last month, Paul had shared with his friends the incredible news of the dream that night in Troas. A man standing by his bedside with pleading eyes, entreating "Paul, please! Come over to Macedonia and help us!" Paul smiled as he recalled the smiles on the faces of Silas, Timothy, and Luke, who had just joined them. They were ready to act on this word from God and take the Good News of Jesus to far away lands. They had fresh vigor in their hearts as they sailed to Neapolis and then walked the rest of the way to the outskirts of Philippi. There they found Lydia, among others, worshiping the true God and hungry to hear of this news of the Lord Jesus Christ. They baptized her there at the river, along with her entire family. Everything

TARSUS

PHILIPI

ROME

TROAS

THESSALONICA

CAPPADOCIA

GALATIA

MACEDONIA

ANTIOCH

EPHESUS

SYRIA

ASIA

ITALY

SICILY

MEDITERRANEAN SEA

EGYPT

CORINTH

CAESAREA

JERUSALEM

ATHENS

from Paul's dream seemed to unlock the most glorious possibilities. Nothing was preventing them from being Christ's witnesses.

And then Paul had seen her: Atalante, the slave girl who could tell people's fortunes thanks to that wild demonic spirit within her. She had no hope, controlled by her selfish owners. All Paul had planned to do yesterday was to pray and preach about Jesus. And then, like she had done for several days already, Atalante called out that Paul and Silas knew the true God of salvation. That spirit must come out, thought Paul, and his rebuke of the demon soon followed. Atalante was whole again; her owners' income would not be. And that's when they attacked Paul and Silas with the crowd. Now they were here in the jail.

Paul opened his eyes.

"Well, Silas, I fear this won't be the last time we are treated in this fashion, but think of what we can praise God for instead. Like how faithful Jesus is to His promises."

"What do you mean?"

Paul shifted himself as well as he could. "It's something Peter told me when I stayed with him in Jerusalem a few years ago. He was there when Jesus ascended into heaven and the Lord told him and the other apostles that they would be His witnesses in Jerusalem, in all Judea, to Samaria, and then to the ends of the earth!"

"And what is it you're trying to say?"

"When we arrived here in Macedonia from Troas, we didn't just cross the Aegean Sea. We showed Jesus' promises are coming true. When we baptized Lydia, her family, and many others we saw repentance and faith on the river banks from people touched with the message of Christ...we're doing it! We are making followers of Jesus in increasingly remote territory! We are taking salvation in Jesus to the ends of the earth."

Silas nodded his head in agreement. "It's true, what you say. His promises are coming true."

Paul shifted again. "We can trust Christ even in the darkness of this cell. Even nearing midnight, the darkness does not overcome the grace of God."

"That is something worth singing about," said Silas.

"All praise to you, our Lord and God
Who left the heavens and came
To live with us and born as us
Renouncing heaven's fame
As man you humbled thus yourself
Obedient unto death
Yet raised to life, above all names
We praise you with our breath."[1]

The singing continued, with Silas' deep rumble bolstering Paul's melodic range. They had kept their voices low at first, but then they were surprised when the prisoners in the outer cell heard them and asked them to continue. After several minutes, one of the prisoners began weeping.

"What is it?" called Paul.

The prisoner sniffled loudly. "My son! He's in the army and I am so fearful for his safety. And when he left home, he and I argued so fiercely that we parted on bad terms. I am ashamed and so afraid I'll never see him again."

"I don't know where he is, my friend," Paul said reassuringly, "but I do know the Lord Jesus Christ, and I know Jesus listens to prayer. Can I pray for you and your son?"

"Yes!" sobbed the prisoner in the darkness.

Paul began to pray aloud, the cries and sniffles continuing from the outer cell. And although he could not see anything in the dark, Paul suddenly felt it. A wobble, then a tremor.

---

1. Philippians 2 authors paraphrase.

"What is that?" called out one of the prisoners.

"Is the city under attack?" yelled another.

"I don't think that's what it is," Paul replied, "This sound is coming from beneath us."

A giant snapping from below confirmed Paul's words, and he could hear the other prisoners screaming for the jailer.

"Paul," Silas whispered next to him. "I think we might be..."

Paul never heard what followed out of Silas' mouth, for the loud crack and violent roar of shifting stones brought the roof of the cell crashing in pieces around them!

With the greatest effort, the jailer, Ontarius shoved the door off his prone body, splinters, rocks, and dust falling everywhere. His torch had been extinguished amongst the destruction. He reached for the table so he could pull himself up, and that's when he saw it. The moon. Shining clearly through a gaping gash in the prison wall.

The doors are opened, Ontarius realized. The earthquake must have split the prison apart! The prisoners are likely all free!

"Hello!" he called into the darkness. Nothing. Not even the slightest cough.

Ontarius was certain that the prisoners must have all escaped. Even one escape meant he was solely responsible. And he knew the law's requirement. He thought of his wife and how she would have to witness his execution now. That he would never see his children grow up. He could not allow them to witness their father's humiliation.

His hand grasped his sword and drew it out of its sheath. Pressing it below his chin, he whispered a final prayer when a voice rang through the grime and the gloom.

"Don't harm yourself!"

Ontarius expelled a loud gasp from his throat. That voice, he racked his mind. "Paul?" he gasped.

"Yes! The earthquake has loosed our stocks, so Silas and I have crawled into the main cell to check on the others. Their chains have also snapped, but we are all here! Please, do not do anything rash! Bring others and see for yourself."

The ringing in Ontarius' ears had muffled the clarity of Paul's speech, but he still understood every word. Shaking himself, Ontarius stumbled to the iron door, now a twisted set of stakes, and called through. "Ho! Guards! Bring lights and water to the holding cell!" Tottering over the rubble he eventually found Paul tending to one of prisoners with a bloody gash on his forehead.

Paul looked up and explained, "This wound will need treatment."

"He's not the only one," Ontarius huffed unevenly. "Look at your face, your arms!"

Ontarius barked out orders as other guards entered the cell. "You there, see to these prisoners. Let none escape, but treat them well and tend to their wounds." He turned to Paul and Silas. "Come with me. Silas, let me help bear your weight. I thought all of you had left."

"None did," Paul replied when they had sat down out of the way of the rubble, "and our Lord Jesus has kept us all alive."

At the name of Jesus, Ontarius dropped to his knees. From somewhere deep within, a groaning sob broke loose. Pitching forward, he fell at Paul's feet, and Paul and Silas quickly drew to either side and embraced Ontarius as he wailed.

"There is no need to fear, Ontarius," Silas said quietly.

"There is every reason," said the jailer, "because for the first time in my life, I realize how lost in spirit I truly am, how hopeless I have come to be."

He looked at the two of them, tears glistening in the moonlight. "Sirs, what must I do to be saved?"

Paul grinned broadly, placing his hand on Ontarius' shoulder and speaking words that were music to the guard's heart. "Ontarius, believe in the Lord Jesus, and you will be saved."

"In Jesus?"

"Yes, by Him and in Him, you will be saved. And not only you," Paul paused. "Would this not be good news for your entire family?"

For the first time in his life, Ontarius felt hope. "Jesus. Yes. And if He has kept you safe now, surely He would save me and my dear ones." He wiped the grime from his face. "Guards! Tend to the rest of these prisoners kindly." He stood gingerly and beckoned Paul and Silas. "Paul, let's get Silas between us and go."

"Go where?" asked Paul.

"To my home for something to eat," Ontarius smiled. "So I can tend to your wounds and wash you both clean, and you can tell me and my family how we might receive this Jesus."

PAUL's story is another dramatic triumph of God's grace. A zealous persecutor of Christians, Paul encountered the risen Jesus in person when traveling to Damascus to arrest Christian believers there. Through that incident, Paul embraced Jesus as Lord and Savior and became a missionary to take the good news of Christ's Gospel as far and wide as he could. This story from Philippi (found in Acts 16) resulted in the beginning and growth of a dynamic, joyful church in Philippi after Paul and Silas' release. Paul would continue his missionary travels—returning again to Philippi—on several more journeys before going to Rome. There, this champion of the Gospel would be executed in the persecution under the Emperor Nero.

FACT FILES

Persecution in the Ancient Church

The ancient Christians shared many experiences together. Luke tells us in Acts 2 that they were fully committed to the teaching of the apostles and to praying together. Christians also worshiped together in groups and met in one another's homes for meals. In order that no one should be lacking basic needs, they gave generously to the poor and to widows. And yet, there was one experience that became more common as the years passed: persecution.

Jesus told His disciples, who became the original apostles, that they would be persecuted, afflicted with unimaginable cruelty due to their faith in Him. Jesus said in John 15:18-19 that "if the world hates you, know that it has hated me before it hated you...I chose you out of the world, therefore the world hates you." Thus, the early Christians could be encouraged that persecution had a way of showing they were authentic believers whom Christ loved. However, the cruelty of the persecution would leave Christians quite distressed in body and spirit. Torture and death—like that of Stephen in Acts 7—were definite possibilities for the ancient Church.

What was it that motivated those who committed persecution? In some cases, like when Jewish religious leaders afflicted the Christians, it was because of the message of Jesus as the resurrected Messiah and giver of salvation. However, much of the persecution of ancient times occurred on the watch of Roman emperors, who had various motivations. There were some rulers who hated Jesus and His followers, but ordinarily, Roman emperors did not mind if people worshiped Jesus Christ; the problem for Rome was that the Christians would only worship Jesus and would never admit that Rome's many gods were legitimate. Praying and sacrificing to gods like Zeus, Mars, and others were means by which the Roman Empire's safety and security was preserved, or so the Romans thought. When Christians refused to bow down to these gods, the Romans accused them of treason against the Empire.

Christian believers had to face the savagery of Nero (reigned from 54-68), who had both Peter and Paul put to death. Paranoid that members of his family would wrest the kingdom from him, he killed his mother Agrippina and also executed his first wife Octavia. A great fire swept through Rome in 64, and when Nero was suspected of starting the blaze, he blamed the Christians for it. This began a great persecution when Nero ordered some Christians to be fed to starving dogs and others crucified in Rome's streets, set on fire to give light after sundown. Despite the martyrdom of these believers (those who are killed for their faith are called martyrs), the Christian church continued to grow and spread.

Nero—driven to insanity—eventually committed suicide, but one of his successors, Domitian (81-96), returned to the policy of persecuting Christians. Proclaiming that he was divine, Domitian would order the execution of Christians who refused to worship him, labeling them "atheists" and "traitors". Soon after Domitian, the emperor Trajan (98-117) ascended the throne. The bishop of Antioch, Ignatius, met his death under the reign of Trajan (we will tell Ignatius' story in chapter 3), but overall, Trajan's policy of persecution was more measured than those of Nero or Domitian. While local governors desired to hunt down Christians for trial and torture, Trajan advised them to take a more generous approach. Trajan did not want the chaos of continued unrest in his empire, preferring to extend order and security quietly so people would see him as a competent ruler. He ordered that Christians should face arrest only if their activity had become too public or stubborn, and so local rulers did not need to seek out Christians.

Marcus Aurelius (161-180), preferred philosophy, poetry, and peace, and so the persecution of Christians was not an issue he dealt with directly. He allowed local governors to enforce policy against Christians, and for some time, persecution increased during his reign. During the third century A.D., Christians found themselves under more systematic persecution. During the reign of Decius (249-251), all citizens of the Empire had to show proof they had sacrificed to the gods or they would be tortured before facing a brutal death. When Cyprian (in chapter 5) was bishop of Carthage, he had to make difficult decisions about Christians who sacrificed to Roman gods to stay alive and then wanted to return to the Church once persecution passed. Diocletian (284-305) unleashed the most brutal persecution of all, casting Christians from their homes, destroying their churches, and burning their books and other literary works.

Many Christians lost home, health, and life during these persecutions. And yet, the Church grew and expanded. In many places in the book of Acts, we find that in the midst of persecution, "the word of God continued to increase and prevail mightily." (Acts 19:20, also see 6:7 and 12:24) The ancient Christian teacher Tertullian forcefully declared that "the blood of the martyrs is the seed of the church." No matter how much persecution the followers of Jesus shall face, Tertullian stated, the Church will continue to grow and thrive against all odds.

Finally, the peace that so many Christians longed for arrived in the reign of Constantine. Preparing to fight his rival Maxentius at the Battle of the Milvian Bridge, Constantine peered into the sky and viewed a cross adorned with the words, "In this sign, you will conquer."

His victory in the battle convinced him that the Christian God had granted him the victory, and Constantine eliminated all persecution against Christians throughout his realm. He followed this with the Edict of Milan in 313, which granted Christians full liberties throughout the Empire, restored their property to them, and legalized the worship of Jesus Christ in all Roman lands.

And yet the liberty given to Christians would bring about challenges of its own. Persecution remains a factor throughout the world today. In the last century, more Christians have been martyred for their faith than all the preceding years of human history. The need to pray for God's grace in this present darkness is as strong as ever.

IGNATIUS

AD 110, between Ostia Antica and Rome

"Stop here," ordered the captain, tapping the boulder with the butt of his spear, offering a spot in the late afternoon shade to the traveling party. The soldiers circled around and dismounted from their horses as two other men, dressed simply in their dusty tunics, shuffled toward the boulder and sat down gingerly.

The captain nodded to one of his subordinates, who produced a skin of water and an amphora of wine for the two travelers. "Drink, Ignatius. You too, Burrhus. We are just three leagues from the gates of Rome, so we might reach it just before nightfall. There is also some bread in these pouches. This will fortify you for the final push of our journey."

"I must say," replied Ignatius, "that it has been quite the journey, good sir. Navigating the ship into the harbor at Ostia took a great deal of skill."

"That harbor is so silted over that Emperor Trajan has declared the need to build a new one in the next few years. It will be hexagonal in shape, which is a good idea. That way, it will reduce the force of the waves against the shore and prevent as much erosion."

"Regardless, the sailors did well at that harbor. And regarding the whole journey, I thank you for taking such good care of us and protecting us at every turn."

The captain patted the nose of his steed before turning back to Ignatius. "The fact that you are so thankful, and expressively so every day, when you know what awaits you in Rome absolutely befuddles me, Ignatius. How can you be so calm and so kind given these circumstances? We have escorted you to your certain death! Why do you treat us as friends?"

"It's a question I have been wondering, too, Ignatius," mumbled Burrhus.

"Burrhus, our lives are so short anyway, when we consider the truth," Ignatius responded. "The least I can do is show kindness to others as Jesus Christ showed kindness and mercy to me who deserved only the wrath and displeasure of God! This is the end to which I was appointed, my friends. Do not be baffled."

The Captain shook his head. "I'm even more baffled by your Christ than I am by your demeanor." Desperate to change the subject, he saw two soldiers leading their horses to the nearby Tiber for a drink. "Ho, men! I'll join you with my horse!" And he disappeared.

Ignatius frowned as he saw them vanish toward the river. "Pity. I would have liked for him to remain so we could speak more about the Savior. We at least have had the opportunity to speak of our risen Lord within earshot of our captors," Ignatius smiled warmly. "So, for that reason it has been a blessing to have a military escort. I often wondered why I wasn't killed in Antioch. It is my home. It is where I have served Christ with all my heart. And if the governor Justus had remained instead of traveling abroad, I would have met my end there. But the legate who oversaw Antioch during Justus' absence could pronounce sentence but not carry out the execution," Ignatius explained, leaning back on the grass. "In the end, it was just as well. If I had been martyred there, the church might have gone into a frenzy. I want them to always have the Gospel of Christ before them, not the memory of their leader. And I was able to name my successor. Heron will be a godly and humble one to walk in my steps as I walked in the steps of

Christ. Don't forget, Burrhus, that it is an honor to come to the place where the fathers of our faith, Peter and Paul, both met their end."

Burrhus nodded but looked down, a thoughtful and disturbed look crossing his face.

"Do you not believe me, my son?" asked Ignatius.

"I want to," Burrhus said. "I am just amazed that I was allowed to accompany you from Ephesus after you arrived there. How can you be so calm? If I was standing in your sandals, I know I wouldn't be! Yet, after we part at the gates of Rome, I'll be released to return back home! And that truth makes me ashamed." A tear trickled down Burrhus' cheek.

Ignatius sat up, leaning toward Burrhus and placing his hand upon his shoulder. "My son, you have nothing to be ashamed of. If God has continued use for you on earth, why should you weep about that? I will see His glory in heaven. Don't be ashamed that we have different paths, for that is the Lord's choosing. He still has work for you to do to strengthen the saints here."

"I don't see how."

Ignatius squeezed Burrhus' arm. "You are a fine deacon. The church at Ephesus is blessed to have you and your gifts. And I know that because you have a wonderful and godly bishop there. He chose you carefully; he chose you well. And he knows, as I do, that what is needed is not that you labor unscathed, but faithfully."

"I pray that will always remain the case."

"Burrhus," Ignatius replied, "do you remember when we stopped in Troas and spent the night in that upper room before sailing to Philippi the next day?"

"I remember," Burrhus said with a faraway look in his eyes. "You said you had to sit and write, that you must write Polycarp, because there were things you needed to say that didn't get said when you saw him in Smyrna."

"Indeed, and I penned words to him that I would use now to you. Stand firm, as does an anvil which is beaten. It is the part of a noble athlete to be wounded, and yet to conquer. And especially, we ought to bear all things for the sake of God, that He also may bear with us. That is where I pray you will take your stand, with no reason to be ashamed."

Burrhus looked over to the Tiber, where the soldiers had turned to come back to their bivouac. "Ignatius, so much of what we know as Christians is changing. Our churches grow despite heavy attack and persecution. It seems that the more our rulers try to stamp us out, the more numerous we become. I rejoice at this...and yet..."

Ignatius nodded as a breeze floated by. "You are wondering if this is sustainable. That is only natural. I would remind you that this is the church of Christ. He sustains it. He rules it. He directs it. Certainly, we should have no fear if that is the case."

"Yes, I believe that with all my heart, Ignatius. It's just that we don't see Jesus in the flesh as I see you here before me. So often, I see our circumstances more clearly. I know that is my own lack of faith, but so much of our time in Ephesus is taken up with people coming in and attacking the bishop and the elders there. People who deny the good gifts God has granted us to be enjoyed. People who say Jesus is a shapeless amorphous spirit, nothing more. It is so difficult to climb out of bed in the morning when I know of the battles that will assail us until I sleep again."

"All of which," Ignatius replied firmly but kindly, raising a single finger for emphasis, "you knew of when Gaius ordained you as a deacon. You are to serve in pleasant times and in times of war. Remember the words of the prophet Isaiah, that when we go through the waters and deep rivers, the Lord will be with us and the waves will not cover us. When we trudge through fire, we will not be burned, because the Holy One is our Savior."[1]

Burrhus looked pensive, took a sip of wine, and asked, "Ignatius, what do you say we should do? I am to go back to Ephesus to serve Christ for the remainder of my life. You are facing your death in days, and you can look back on many years of serving our Lord. What do we need to prepare for?"

Ignatius took the drinking jar from him and set it between them before tossing the pouch of bread alongside it. "Many false teachings will arise. You should expect that. You have seen the effects of them already in Ephesus, Burrhus. Of course, that only demonstrates the truth of what the apostles have said. Paul warned you these savage false teachers would come. The followers of the Lord Jesus Christ must hold together. Love unity, and flee from division."

Ignatius paused, and Burrhus thought he looked slightly troubled, but the bishop smiled and continued. "Above all, as I've said before, turn a deaf ear to anyone who does not accept Jesus of King David's line and born of Mary. Yes, Jesus is divine, but we must always remember that we as sinners need Him to be human to take our sins for us. Never forget that Jesus ate and drank as we do, that He really died and His body was raised. And He will raise us one day...one day." Ignatius turned his head slightly, looking northeast toward Rome. The Colosseum, Burrhus thought. He is preparing to die well even now.

"I pray I can play my own part in helping others to be faithful to Christ, Ignatius," Burrhus whispered. His tears were beginning to flow freely now.

"There is one thing you can always remind them of, my son," Ignatius responded. "In following our Lord Jesus, in combating falsehood and the wolves of crooked doctrine

1. Isaiah 43:2-3.

that would lead the sheep astray, remember the steadfast love of God. Those whom you teach and lead might forget your words and eloquence, but they will remember how you teach, how you lead, how you exhort, how you rebuke, how you build them up. Call out their sins, but do so from a heart that beats as Christ's heart does for them. Love them as Jesus does."

The Captain stopped next to them in the grass, his stallion shaking his mane and sending droplets of water from his drink in the Tiber everywhere. "My apologies for that, travelers." He looked in the distance toward Rome. "I would advise you to take your food and drink if you haven't yet. We will be leaving in a quarter hour's time to enter the city tonight."

He walked off, leaving the two Christians together seated on the grass. Deacon and bishop. A young preacher and one in his prime. A minister soon to return to his earthly home and one ready for his eternal home. Burrhus looked at the pouch of bread and the wine between them and looked at Ignatius.

"This could be our last meal together, my friend," he said.

Ignatius nodded. "How fitting that I can enjoy this meal with you this fine evening." He broke the bread with a quick turn of his wrists and gave Burrhus his portion of it. They both ate of the bread before Ignatius raised the container of wine in his hands. "My friend, this is the medicine of immortality.[2] Christ has died, Christ is risen, Christ will come again." He took a long drink and then passed it to Burrhus, who drank, as well.

"To come to this place, and break the bread of the Eucharist with you, my father..." Burrhus wept, the tears flooding down his face.

"Take courage for your future, my son," Ignatius smiled as the soldiers approached. Raising the final morsel of

2. Taken from Ignatius' *Epistle to the Ephesians.*

bread in his right hand, he grasped Burrhus' hand for one more prayer. "May Jesus be present in my death as He has been throughout my life. Suffer me to be eaten by the beasts, through whom I can attain to God. I am God's wheat, to be ground by the teeth of beasts that I may be found to be the pure bread of Christ."[3]

"Amen," croaked Burrhus, and the two men looked up to find the captain standing over them, a glint of a tear in his eye.

"Ignatius, Burrhus, it is time."

The door creaked open as Ignatius stood in the Colosseum, the wild beasts unleashed from behind the far gate. The sun was bright overhead, with a slight wind from the sea. Burrhus has a beautiful day to travel back home, thought Ignatius. He looked at the crowds, their voices roaring from the stands, but as the animals charged, he kept looking upward beyond the top of the Colosseum. Uttering a final prayer, he saw his Savior, waiting to receive him.

IGNATIUS served as the bishop of Antioch in Syria. An important link between the New Testament apostles and the remainder of early church history, Ignatius wrote one of the earliest creeds (short statements of Christian belief) in which he defended Jesus' divine and human nature. He never tired of urging Christians to love one another well, to show respect and obedience to bishops charged with their spiritual nurture, and to remain faithful to Christ. On his final journey toward his martyrdom in Rome, he wrote seven letters to churches, which are among the earliest writings and most glorious treasures of the second-century church. They reveal a heart burning for Christ that was resolved to follow Him to death.

3. Taken from Ignatius' letter to the Romans. https://christianhistoryinstitute.org/incontext/article/ignatius

POLYCARP

AD 155, Smyrna

"Polycarp!" Camerius hissed. "There is a knock at the door!"

The aged bishop looked up, his sop of bread left in the bowl of stew as Camerius hid below the window and his wife scurried under the table as the knocks came, harder and further apart.

Polycarp sighed. He had gone to the country because his people had judged it best. But how could they remain a church without their bishop to guide them? With a groan Polycarp placed his hands on the table and looked at his friend.

"No, Camerius," he whispered back. "There is no reason for me to hide anymore! I beg you to answer your door and let the soldiers in. Perhaps Myra, your wife, has some of stew and bread ready if the guards are hungry."

"But Polycarp..."

"No, my friend. I believe this is what the Holy Spirit is directing me to do. I might go, but the Spirit will always dwell in your midst. Please open the door."

Wide-eyed and disbelieving, Camerius gingerly raised himself up from his crouched position. Opening the door, he blinked at the bright sunshine and the sight of six Roman guards standing there.

"You are Camerius, owner of this farm?" The captain barked, flecks of spit on his chin.

"I am, sire."

"I am Porcius, the captain of the guard. We have reason to believe you are sheltering one named Polycarp, the bishop of Christians in this region of Smyrna. We have orders from the judge Herod to come quickly to the city center, where he is to offer sacrifice to our gods."

Camerius began to protest but Polycarp gently laid his hand on his friend's arm to stop him.

"Ah, captain. How good of you to come with your men...."

"We must bring you to the city, Polycarp. You are charged to come," the captain replied, stone-faced.

"Yes, I understand, and I will come in due course," Polycarp replied. "But it seems to me that if you and your men have marched all this way from the city, you must be ravenously hungry. Would you care for a small meal before we make our return?"

Porcius' face blanched, overcome with complete surprise. "It...it would have to be brief," he stammered. Looking into the dining area, he continued, "and we would have difficulty fitting all our men around your table."

"Please, captain," Myra replied, "if you could join us at table, I can serve your men and they can take their meal outdoors."

"You should know," the captain mumbled between bites of soggy, stew-sopped bread, "that the judge has those who would seek out Christians and torture them to discover your hiding places."

"Is that how you found me?" Polycarp asked him quietly.

Porcius nodded.

Polycarp shook his head. "Only two people knew exactly where I would go. And they were members of my own household."

"Herod's men would say they were only doing their job to extract their knowledge," Porcius said dourly. "I can tell you many who held out and would not speak a word."

"Which meant someone broke under pressure," Polycarp replied. "I do not think less of anyone for that. It is as the

Lord wills. You are not going to report my benefactors here, are you?"

The captain looked at the two hosts, who had joined hands in fear. "No," he said, "I can say we found you but I do not have to be excessively detailed in my report." He then turned to Camerius and his wife. "But you both need to be careful. If you are part of this Christian sect as Polycarp is, that is for you to bear. I cannot defend you if you are too public in your worship. And if Herod hears of you and demands you sacrifice to the gods, you have a decision to make."

"But you will not arrest us for shielding Polycarp?" Camerius asked.

"No. You and your farm will be untouched."

"Speaking of their farm, good captain, Camerius' storage barn has a damaged roof. Don't you have a brother who repairs houses and barns?"

"Yes, I do," Porcius nodded. He looked at his hosts. "Do you need it repaired? I can ask him."

"Oh, I could not impose..." Camerius began.

"It would be my honor. Your wife's stew will strengthen my men on the way home, so consider this evening the scales. I'll speak with him upon my return, provided all is well with him."

"What do you speak of?" Polycarp asked.

The captain shook his head. "My niece is very ill. She cannot keep her meals down, cannot gain weight, and her hair is thinning. It is difficult for them to bear, difficult for me as her uncle to think about..." He stopped eating, his eyes filling with tears.

Polycarp reached across the table and laid his hand on the captain's shoulder. "Whatever the divide between you and me, I would ask to pray for child right now."

"I will not stop you, Polycarp."

Polycarp bowed his head. "I beg you, O Lord Jesus, our Master, to help and protect this young girl. Save her in her affliction, have mercy upon her, and raise her up to health. Appear to her and save her soul, giving her rest from her wanderings. Raise her up, we pray, O Lord our Savior, from sickness, and comfort her evermore in the name of the Father, Son, and Holy Spirit. Amen."

The room was completely quiet. Silent tears poured down the captain's face. Polycarp turned to Camerius and Myra, and spoke to them one last time.

"It is time for me to go, my friends. God be with you, for He, not I, is with you forever."

Polycarp was set upon a donkey, who wobbled forth into the heart of Smyrna bearing his weight. The sweet animal made no complaint as they neared the chariot that held Herod and his father Nicetes. Suddenly, Polycarp heard a sigh to his right. It was Porcius, his face quite sad.

"Please forgive me, Polycarp, for I don't know what I am doing!"

Polycarp spoke briskly and quietly. "I do, and moreover, so does the Lord Jesus, far more than you could possibly imagine."

"Ho, Polycarp!" came a sneering voice from the chariot. Behind it, the stadium was filled to capacity with roaring citizens.

Polycarp gently pulled the reins on the donkey. "Yes, my lord Herod. You wish to see me?"

"To give you one chance to save yourself before the flames of death, you evil man!" Herod spat. "Get in!"

"There is no need to save myself," Polycarp responded gently as he climbed painfully into the chariot. 'The Lord Jesus has already done so when He died and rose from the dead.."

"Silence, patterer!" roared Herod as he drew himself to his full height, his paunchy middle bulging under his toga. "Polycarp, the bishop of the Christian rabble of Smyrna, I ask you this: What harm is there in saying 'Lord, Caesar!', in sacrificing to the many gods beyond your sole deity, in joining the rhythm of ceremonies we observe, and thus making your safety certain?"

Polycarp smiled. Lord, the pain of death will be great, he thought, but to see your face is greater wonder than that. He met Herod's glare with kind eyes and a firm tone. "No, Herod. I shall not do as you advise me."

So focused had he been on meeting Herod's eyes that he never saw the kick come from the guard to his right. Polycarp felt his ribs cave in from the blow as he fell from the chariot. He hit the ground at an awkward angle and felt something pop as the dust swirled around him. The searing pain shot down his leg and elicited a cry from his mouth.

"Get him up!" Herod ordered the soldiers. "He's only dislocated his creaky hip. Bring him into the stadium and he will know what true anguish is!"

Even the soldiers marveled that, after a few steps, Polycarp was able to hobble along eagerly, as if he could not wait to stand before the stadium's throng. As they entered the tumult, Herod had to call for quiet, for no one could hear above the din of the crowd.

Except that Polycarp could. As he shuffled toward the stake placed in the center of the arena, he heard a still, small voice. "Be strong, O Polycarp, and show yourself a man." The pagans around him paid no heed, and he wondered if he had heard the voice at all. Then he saw Camerius. And Myra. And others on the end of the stadium. They had also heard it, he knew. And then his eyes rested on Irenaeus, head bowed in prayer in the third row of the west side. *Father God, be with dear Irenaeus,* Polycarp prayed, *keep him bold as he shepherds your flock and may he be strong to his own difficult end.*

The crowd quieted as Herod raised his hands and then gestured to Statius Quadratus, the governor. The swaggering ruler swept in front of Polycarp, fist high to the heavens, and called out, "Old man, have respect for your years, and offer sacrifices to the gods!"

"Obey him!" cried a man from the north of the stadium.

"Deny your false God!" screamed a woman from the south end.

Polycarp looked at the assembly as the sun peeked out from behind the clouds. "My years are as they are. But it is Christ who has faithfully led me through them!"

The crowd erupted with rage, save the few Christians sprinkled in their midst. The proconsul raised his hands to silence them.

"Listen to the mob!" he snapped at Polycarp. "You deluded dotard, refusing to pay homage to the gods whom we honor! It is you who deny the deities, you atheist. Swear by the good will of Caesar; repent and say of your kind, 'Away with the atheists!'"

The crowd began to stomp, giddy with bloodthirst. Polycarp raised his hand and gestured at the crowds in the stadium. With an unexpected booming voice, he declared, "No, it is the ones who accuse me today! Away with them! Away with the atheists!"

If the soldiers had not ringed around the edge of the stadium, the crazed citizens who jumped from the stands might have reached Polycarp to tear him apart. Instead, the governor grabbed Polycarp by the shoulders and shrieked, "You insane son of a demon! Swear now, and I will set you free. Only curse your Christ!"

The shouts in the stadium subsided, everyone straining to hear the bishop's response. What they weren't expecting was for Polycarp to shake himself free and walk toward the stake. Looking up at it, Polycarp blinked back the sweat and tears in his eyes, imagining he could see a beam of wood across the upright piece only for a moment. Taking a deep breath, he turned and addressed the governor, Herod, and the crowd.

"Eighty-six years, men! To the citizens of Smyrna, I say the same! Eighty and six years have I served the Lord Jesus Christ, and He has never done me any harm. How then can I curse and blaspheme my loving King, who saved me? You threaten me with fire which burns for an hour, and after a little is extinguished, but you are ignorant of the fire of the coming judgment and eternal punishment. But why do you delay? Bring forth what you will, and I will meet my Savior!"

Bound to the stake, Polycarp smelled the smoke and saw the flames leap around him. Looking around, he saw once more the praying forms of Camerius, Myra, and Irenaeus when he felt a sharp pain pierce his side.

Raising his eyes to heaven, Polycarp lifted up a final prayer, "Lord God Almighty, I thank you that you have counted me worthy of this day and hour, to be numbered among your martyrs with the cup of Christ to the resurrection of eternal life. Accept my sacrifice, I pray, as I praise you for all things, and bless and glorify you and your everlasting Son, Jesus Christ, to whom, with you and the Holy Spirit, be glory now in my death and throughout all years to come."

He felt his strength and life trickling away, and with the smile of joy blazing from his face, Polycarp mouthed a final "Amen."

POLYCARP served faithfully as the bishop of Smyrna. A disciple of the apostle John, who ordained him as an elder, Polycarp forms an important link between the apostles of the New Testament and the rest of the early Church. He was a correspondent with another martyr, Ignatius of Antioch, and he mentored and shepherded many leaders to come, including Irenaeus, who would become bishop of Lyons. A respected teacher, Polycarp carefully defended biblical teaching against the falsehoods of various heretics. But it is his zeal to give his life as a testimony of God's grace for which he is most remembered.

BLACK SEA
SMYRNA
GALATIA
ASIA MINOR
CYPRUS
ANTIOCH
JERICHO
JERUSALEM
JUDEA

CYPRIAN

AD 258, Carthage, North Africa

The banners fluttered, the red and gold colors buffeted by the wind roaring off the Mediterranean Sea past the waters of Carthage's harbor. Soldiers stood guard throughout the sun-kissed courtyard, flanking the proconsul Galerius Maximus seated on the dais, leaning into the brisk wind. For his part, Galerius was incredulous. Surely he had misheard the words coming from the mouth of his captive! Certainly this raspy, quiet cleric could not have uttered what he did!

"I am sorry," sneered Galerius. "Perhaps you are mistaking me for a more lenient proconsul, Cyprian. I asked you if you will show yourself faithful to Rome and conform to the rites of sacrificing to our gods! No one is asking you to deny your Christ. But we do demand you show obeisance to our gods!"

The bishop stood firm, his limbs shaking and his stomach growling from lack of food, but he would not yield. "My esteemed proconsul, I believe you know not what you say. There is only one King of Heaven, and full—not partial—allegiance is due to him. To affirm Rome's gods is to deny my Lord and Savior Jesus Christ, and this I refuse to do!"

Thousands of citizens crowded the area, gasping as one at the boldness of Cyprian's words and tone. Galerius, unused to such firmness from his prisoners, leaned forward and wagged a pudgy finger toward the bishop.

"Take care, Cyprian," he bellowed. "Are you so confident that you return from exile only to place yourself under judgment now?"

Unmoved, Cyprian spread his chained hands as far as possible, palms up in holy resignation. "Do as you are bid, proconsul. In so clear a case, I will not heed your demands."

Some in the crowd roared in excitement as Galerius called the members of the judicial council around him. When the judges dispersed, Galerius wore a pained look, as if the words he was about to say would cause his great harm. "Cyprian, bishop of the fanatics known as Christians, you have long lived the irreligious life, drawing together numbers of people unlawfully, yourself being an open enemy to the pantheon of gods and the religion of Rome. You have shown grievous enmity to the most sacred Emperors. I have tried ... we have tried to convince you of your error and bring you back into this Empire's good graces, but you have determined to continue as the ringleader of these crimes against the gods. Therefore, we must make an example of you ..." He paused as shrieks and protests rose from others in the crowd, earning threats from the guards. "We will make an example to those whom you have wickedly led, and the authority of our law shall be verified by the shedding of your blood."

Galerius rose from his seat. "It is the sentence of this court that you, O Cyprian, shall be executed with the sword!"

Several cries and wails went up, competing with the cheers of those desiring Cyprian's death. The bishop merely smiled and bowed his head.

"Thanks be to God," he whispered before the guards whisked him away.

Down the streets they dragged him, a right turn followed by a left. Cyprian was being taken outside the city for his martyrdom. *As they did my Lord Jesus*, the bishop told himself. So deep was he in thought that he barely heard his name called from several yards away.

He looked. A window of a small villa.

A child. A little girl. Waving. Waving goodbye.
Sophoniba, ... And then he remembered the day.

It had been a little more than a year before. The courtyard of the villa was lush with green grass after an unexpected three-day spell of summer rains. Cyprian sat on the lawn, his linen robe—bearing the insignia of a cross—wrapped around his tunic, and he looked at the four children seated in a semicircle around him. There was Bodo, a curious lad who asked numerous questions. His friend, Sirom, quietly sat next to him. Sirom's lean, dark features rarely exhibited much emotion, but it was not due to lack of understanding, for he was a studious sort. The two girls who joined them for this day's teaching fiddled with blades of esparto grass, rolling them in their hands. Dido shook her fingers vigorously, releasing the grass through the air, while Sophoniba pressed her palms together reverently, as Cyprian posed another question.

"Tell me, children, if we worship our Lord Jesus, and we follow Him with all our beings, then isn't our worship and devotion enough for that?"

Sirom and Sophoniba held their peace, both knowing this was a leading question. Bodo and Dido raised their hands simultaneously, Bodo with such force that his shoulder joint popped rather loudly.

"It is what He has commanded us, so yes, that is enough," declared Bodo.

"I was going to say likewise," Dido muttered, "for following our Lord's commands is of greatest importance."

"Yes, I have no doubt," replied Cyprian, winking at Sirom and Sophoniba for their rightful restraint. "Perhaps I should make it clearer. Why do you think I chose the word 'enough'?"

"Perhaps to trick us?" Dido said smoothly, wiggling her fingers as if anticipating a sidestep by the bishop.

"Would I trick you?" Cyprian declared in mock alarm. "Let me put it another way and ask the others. Sirom, Sophoniba, does it matter where we worship and follow the Lord Jesus?"

Sophoniba nodded her head twice. "I believe it does. I mean, I cannot recall a teaching that says so exactly. But we always meet together as the church."

"That is very wise, wise beyond your eight years," Cyprian rejoined. "What if I asked this? I'd like to hear Sirom answer: What would happen if we did not gather as a church? What then?"

Sirom wrinkled his brow for a few moments, then spoke slowly but evenly. "If we did not meet together, I don't see how we could call ourselves Jesus' people. We would be a man here, a woman there, a child there. You have spoken about Jesus creating a new family. If we don't meet together, we would not exist as Jesus said."

"Excellent, Sirom!" exclaimed Cyprian. "So then, is it more important to meet together or to worship Jesus?"

"I'd say both are equally important," Bodo burst out. "But I have often wondered: Why can't we merely worship Jesus at sunrise on the shoreline? Why can't we just pray when simply walking through the city streets?"

"We'd like to think we could," Cyprian replied patiently, "but I think we should consider what is lost if we answer your questions with a yes."

"What do you mean?" asked Sophoniba.

"Well, in the winter your father builds a good fire to warm you and any guests in your home. What would happen if one branch was used? Would that give the needed warmth?"

"If you lit it, yes," Bodo agreed.

"But for how long?" asked Sirom.

"Exactly," Cyprian nodded, pleased the truth was starting to take root in the children's minds. "The single branch would burn for a while, but eventually it would go out. What is needed to keep the fire burning?"

"Another branch!" All four shouted excitedly.

"That is true," Cyprian grinned. "Just as your family needs a fire to keep warm Christians need the Good News of our Lord, and the encouragement we receive from other believers. The fire only continues to burn if there is more than one branch. The gospel is only effective if believers join together. We are like the branches in the fire. Only when we are together as the Church will the fire keep burning!"

"So you are saying worshiping God our Father, Jesus His Son, praying to the Holy Spirit...those aren't as important?" Bodo pressed.

"No, Bodo, I simply say that as well as God the Father, God the Son and God the Holy Spirit, our God has also given us the gift of His Church to be a part of. We need our Lord. And we need the Church. You know how wonderful it is to have a father and a mother. God in His wisdom has given us the Church. We need both. This is our family!"

"Is that why you wanted those people to return to the Church?" asked Dido.

"Yes that is correct. I wanted some people to return to the Church, and there was a great argument over how we should do so."

The four children leaned it to hear the story, as the word argument had sparked their curiosity.

"I will only give the smallest of details," Cyprian said, "out of respect for those who disagreed with me, for they are shepherds of Christ's Church as well. Around the time you four were born, there was a great persecution under a ruler named Decius. Terrible things happened, which I shall not explain now, but many followers of our Lord were tortured, and some were killed simply because they professed their love and loyalty to Jesus alone. Others had tried to endure, but the pain of what the emperor's soldiers had done to them was too much. They decided they wanted to live rather than die, and they sacrificed to the Roman gods instead."

"Why did they do that?" exploded Bodo. "If I was suffering for Jesus, I would never do that!" "Bodo, be careful what you say. Remember how we read the story of Peter last week. He had been certain of his bravery. He had to be humbled."

Bodo sat silent, looking slightly embarrassed. Sirom noticed his dour look and gave him an encouraging pat on the shoulder.

Cyprian continued. "One day, the persecution ended, and the Church had peace. There was great discussion and debate about what we should do, for some held that if the lapsed had given up in the face of persecution, they did not deserve to return to the Church. One man, named Novatian, believed this very firmly. I do not speak evil of him; he was only trying to protect the Church in his way. Another bishop, Cornelius from Rome, believed we should allow all the lapsed to return to the churches graciously and not make any demands on them. It was very complicated. I had supported Cornelius to be the new bishop, but I did not believe his allowance for the lapsed was good. And Novatian did not like the fact that I supported Cornelius instead of him. So, I had to tell both men I believed the Lord called for a different approach."

"I was wondering if you would come up with a new idea!" Sirom interjected.

"I didn't believe the lapsed should return to the Church as if what they'd done was a good thing. So many others had suffered and died in the persecution, and that would not be fair. But I did not believe that closing the door of Christ's Church was right, either. What sort of message would that be?"

ILLYRIANS
GALLIC TRIBES
ROME
CARTHAGE
NUMIDIANS

"What do you mean, Cyprian?" asked Sophoniba.

"Think of the disciples. They scattered and left Jesus when He died on the Cross. They needed to be forgiven. In the parable that Jesus told about the Prodigal Son did the father reject the son? No! The son repented for his sin and rebellion against his father, saying, 'Father, I have sinned against heaven and against you!' His father hugged him, kissed him, and received him back! Why should the Church not do the same?"

"Did they agree with you?" asked Sophoniba.

"Many churches in the area of Carthage, at least," said Cyprian. "Many of the lapsed met with me and the elders. They wept, and confessed they should have been stronger. And I tell you all now what I told them: We are all disobedient and prodigal children; we are all in need of the grace of God. When people repent, we must forgive them, since Jesus has already forgiven us."

The children looked thoughtful for several moments, before Sirom broke the silence. "I hope I will love to give God's grace to others as much as I have received it from Jesus."

Cyprian was about to respond with thanks when a messenger arrived with news from Rome.

Two weeks ago, Stephen the bishop of Rome had been celebrating the Eucharist with his congregation. Emperor Valerian had dispatched soldiers to the church where they executed Stephen on the spot. A new persecution had begun.

The messenger was there to warn Cyprian that he could be next and that now was the time to flee.

Cyprian looked back at the children, who wore worried looks on their faces.

If I am called to give my life one day, I will not deny that call of Christ. Cyprian thought to himself.

As he returned towards the children he cut a flower from a bush with the thought, It will grow back. Let us face the time we have left with courage and grace.

Cyprian slowly removed his linen robe, clutching the blindfold in his fingers as those in the crowd either wept, cried, or shouted. The assembly was so thick, there were some climbing trees to gain a proper line of sight. Cyprian began to make his final walk toward the block when he heard a voice call from behind.

"Cyprian!"

He turned. "Sophoniba!" He pleaded with the soldiers, "Permit me a few moments with her!'

The girl cast herself into his arms, weeping quietly. "Cyprian, you are going to be with our Lord."

"I am, dear one. I do not fear. I ask you to serve Him boldly." And in that moment, Cyprian folded his robe and handed it to her.

Sophoniba looked up at him with shining eyes.

She backed away into the crowd as Cyprian turned to face the executioner. Cyprian closed his eyes in a prayer of thanks. "Praise be to you, Lord Christ. Your Church remains in good hands. Your hands."

CYPRIAN served as the bishop of the church at Carthage from 248 until his death in September 258. A skilled teacher and dedicated writer, his story demonstrates amazing durability and grace for the Gospel's sake. He forcefully defended the necessity of Christians to be a part of their church, dedicated to worship and community. Leading Christians through days of severe persecution, Cyprian guided the Church with wisdom and mercy under a firm hand, even when he was exiled in the year before his death. Returning to Carthage, he willingly faced death as a martyr who knew that Jesus was the Good Shepherd who would always guide His Church.

FACT FILES

Canon, Clergy, Creeds, Churchmen

While the growth of Christianity was amazing throughout the time of persecution, its numerical expansion sparked many questions about how the movement could sustain itself. The Christian Church needed an understanding of what and who would guide its people to be faithful to the mission Jesus had called them, to make disciples of all nations. These questions included "What writings are our authority for life given by God?", "Under what leadership should we submit ourselves?", "How might we carefully and clearly define what our beliefs are?", and "Who are the people who can teach us and others the truth about Jesus?"

The answers to these four questions were found in, as we might call them, the four "C's": canon, clergy, creeds, and churchmen.

The word canon comes from the Greek word for "rule", "norm", or "standard". The Church's "canon" referred to the books that were recognized as God's Word, the written work that belonged to Holy Scripture—what we today call the Bible. Some of these books were already clearly viewed as Scripture; the Old Testament books had been recognized and accepted as God's Word for a long time. When Jesus quoted from the Scriptures, it was from the Old Testament.

The New Testament took its final shape over the first four centuries A.D. Some Christians find it difficult to think that the New Testament "evolved" over time, but there is more to this story. First, the Church always believed there were writings that were clearly God's Word which told the story of God's redemption from the time of Jesus onward. That is, they were convinced of the existence of a New Testament canon, even if they had some extended discussions and disagreements about the exact list of those books.

Yes, the process took time. There were disputes over some books that eventually were recognized as Scriptural, and there were others that—although Christians saw value in them—did not fit with what was already clearly Scriptural.

But how did the Church recognize what books should clearly be part of the New Testament Bible? In truth, because it was God's Word, it should reflect God's nature. So, a New Testament book had to pass the consistency test, as God is consistent in His being and character. A book that could be part of the New Testament had to show consistency with the rest of the story of redemption in the Bible. There was also a truth test, because if God is revealed in Jesus, then a New Testament book should be written by someone who knew Jesus or had access to people familiar with Jesus; that is, an apostle or an associate of an apostle. And, it had to pass the accessibility test, because God is infinite and cannot be contained, so a New Testament book should be known fairly well throughout many of the churches of that day, even if it was addressed to a specific group (e.g., Ephesians).

The Church developed a pattern for leadership by looking at how the New Testament books described it. The Church needed ministers who could reflect Jesus' character to the people and who could reshape believers' lives by proclaiming the Scripture to them. To do this, churches had bishops who gave them oversight, elders who gave believers spiritual direction and nurture, and deacons who served the needs of those in the church and community. These are broad categories, and clear assignment of "who does what" is largely undeveloped in the New Testament. What is clear is that ministers were expected to be individuals of consistent and godly moral character. In I Timothy 3, for example, when Paul describes the role of bishops and deacons, he spends more time describing what sort of people they should be than the specific activities they would do.

As the Church grew and matured, another development was the necessity of creeds. Creeds are short statements of doctrine (teaching) that are essential for a group of believers to hold in common. It is helpful to think of creeds as the gates of the Church. They function in two ways: They are points by which people enter the Christian family, and they are walls of defense by which false teaching is barred from the Church. Originally designed primarily as entry statements for new Christians seeking to be baptized with water, creeds later were useful to define the boundary between truth and falsehood. Ignatius of Antioch wrote a short baptismal creed that affirmed that Jesus Christ, along with being perfectly God, was authentically human, as well. The Nicene Creed (discussed in a later chapter) defended the view that Jesus was the eternal, divine Son of God. The Apostles' Creed developed over time out of several other baptismal creeds and formulas, and the Athanasian Creed (which Athanasius did not write, by the way!) demonstrates that God exists as the Trinity of Father, Son, and Holy Spirit.

The early Church was also blessed with great teachers who explained the Bible and what it revealed about God and His followers. These churchmen were often called apologists, and not because they were saying they were sorry for what they believed! A Christian apologist is an individual who explains how Christian truth makes sense. They defend Christianity against the objections of critics. God blessed the early Church with many influential apologists, among whom were Justin Martyr, Tertullian, and Origen.

Justin Martyr (100-165) was a creative thinker. After a chance encounter with an elderly Syrian Christian, Justin left the paganism of his youth behind and began teaching Christianity. However, Justin believed Greek philosophy and Christian theology could be harmonized. Justin also wrote books that defended Christians from false accusations made by pagans, stating that Christians should not bear the brunt of persecution because they are good citizens who worship Jesus quietly and reasonably, obeying the laws of the state. He also declared that Christian teaching was more noble and moral than the pagan ideals throughout the Empire. In another work, he dialogued with a Jewish philosopher named Trypho. This book was partly Justin's autobiography and partly a response to Trypho, who said that it was inconsistent to believe in one God and also believe that Jesus was the Son of God. Eventually, Justin's debates led to his martyrdom; one of his other critics reported him to the authorities for trial, and Justin was sentenced to death by beheading.

Tertullian (155-240) was born in Carthage in North Africa in the latter part of Justin's life. He is well-known for a high volume of writing after his conversion to the Christian faith in his forties. His sudden change may have affected his belief that a Christian life begins in a radical moment of sudden faith. He was fond of saying, "Christians are made, not born," meaning that one experiences a moment of clear faith rather than being considered a Christian since birth. He wrote widely on apologetics and answering pagan questions, how the Church should function, and the discipline and morality of the Christian life. Some pagans accused Christians of horrendous crimes like sacrificing infants when they celebrated Holy Communion. Tertullian easily disproved these charges, showing Christians to be people committed to the moral law of God. He was the first Christian leader to use the term Trinity when speaking of the Christian God. He held to a strict moral code, which some people found strenuous, and he condemned fleeing from persecution while also stating widows should never remarry. Although he generally admired Justin's work, Tertullian rebelled against Justin's model of finding common ground between Greek philosophy and Christianity, famously declaring, "What does Athens have to do with Jerusalem? What does the academy have to do with the Church?"

Origen's life (185-254) overlapped with Tertullian, but he grew up well east of him, in Alexandria, Egypt. He was born to Christian parents and his father Leonides was martyred when Origen was a teenager. Resolute, Origen eventually dedicated himself to a holy life and serious study and his teacher Clement found Origen to be his most dynamic and creative student. As the years passed, Origen was known for several controversies. His mind was so overzealous and speculative that he wrote a vast number of commentaries on whole books of the Bible, from Genesis to Matthew, from Song of Solomon to Titus. He preferred to interpret Scripture in allegorical ways rather than in a straightforward fashion. But he was well-equipped to battle against any critics and take on all questions, both in apologetic works like Against Celsus and his major work, First Principles, in which he presented an orderly explanation of Christian theology so believers could understand what the Bible revealed about the Triune God.

CONSTANTINE

October 27-28, 312, outside Rome

"We are camping here?" the centurion asked, more loudly than he intended.

Constantine lowered his hand and dismounted from his horse. "Indeed, we are, good Silvanus. Spread the word throughout the legion that we encamp here tonight. We have had many hard days of marching and I want the troops to take food and drink tonight toward a good rest. We do not know what awaits us tomorrow."

"Isn't that an even better reason to keep marching to the gates of Rome? Given what Maxentius has done before?"

"There are reasons for that, Silvanus, but I am concerned with the men's fitness first, which needs to be in place before we consider our enemy's strategy," Constantine acknowledged. "But your point is well-taken." He brushed his hands through his sweaty, wavy hair. "Send me two in your company whom you would trust to be decisive, clear-headed, and yet stealthy. A little reconnaissance would not harm our chances at all."

"I know just the men, my lord. And, sire?"

"Yes, Silvanus?"

"The gods be praised, the Unconquered Sun above all. You have led us well, all the way from Britannia. Our impending victory will be a sweet feast indeed."

Constantine smiled as Silvanus bowed and left. Turning his face toward the River Tiber, some four miles away, he took stock of all his army had accomplished this year as the battle for control of the Roman Empire raged. The crossing of the Mont Cenis pass in the early spring with his forty thousand. The siege of Turin, where Maxentius had sent his forces but had himself stayed behind in Rome, was a joyous memory. Constantine recalled how his more lightly armored cavalry had maneuvered rapidly through and around the confused enemy. Turin had fallen, and then it was on to Verona, another resounding victory in which Ruricius Pompeianus had been slain, leaving Maxentius without a senior general and the path to Rome more secure. The cities of Umbria and Etruria hailed him as emperor, and surging onward, Constantine and his soldiers had enjoyed an unmolested march to the outskirts of Rome itself. They were on the verge of uniting the entire western portion of the Empire under his rule. He stood on the hilltop as the army, well behind him, set up camp. Constantine closed his eyes.

So many successes, he thought, and now I am on the cusp of my greatest victory ever. At last, there can be peace and I can unite this greatest kingdom on earth. Every day I proclaim our steps are guided by divine help. He frowned and swallowed hard. So why do I feel such emptiness inside?

"My lord?" a voice spoke behind him.

Constantine turned. "Aelius. Celsus. Silvanus sent you both. Praise God."

"You need us to spy for you this evening, my lord?" asked Celsus. Both men came lightly armored with swords and shields.

"I do. My command is that you skirt the trees of the forest and stay out of sight from any in the enemy. Perhaps wait until the sun goes completely down to ensure your safety. I want you to see if there are any movements of Maxentius' troops, and if so, where? Do they stay near the gates of the city? Do they approach the Tiber instead? And then report back to Silvanus, who shall report to me."

"My lord," replied Aelius, "we will do so willingly, but it seems that Maxentius would not risk a foray into open territory outside the city walls. Word is he has been stockpiling food, and that suggests he anticipates a siege."

"He did the same with prior invasions, sire," added Celsus. "But we will do as you say."

"It may come to nothing," Constantine agreed, "but the priests might direct Maxentius otherwise, and he listens to the gods as closely and desperately as he can. Well, off with both of you, and take care to yourselves!"

Aelius and Celsus bowed and then walked away in the direction of the forest. Constantine watched them go until he could track them no longer in the tricky light of the setting sun. It was when they disappeared into the trees and he turned back toward a final look into the sky that he saw it.

What is that? Constantine thought. The sky had been getting darker, but there was something unusual in the sky that drew Constantine's attention. There is something odd about the sun! He shielded his eyes and looked more closely. He gazed back at the camp, amazed that no one else saw this phenomenon! He peered back at the sun again and dropped his hands to his sides, staring into the orange ball of light, overcome at what he beheld.

What is that? he marveled. *Why that symbol? And what is that message it bears?*

Sleep that night was a fitful event for Constantine. Thrashing about on his pallet, he could not shake the image of that cross and the imposed letters in the middle of the sun. *Must there be a reason?* He asked himself. *Is there a lesson, a strategy for tomorrow?* So many questions, then he felt, more than heard, a noise in the tent.

Starting from his prone position, Constantine grabbed his sword and flashed it in front of him, crouching low. No one else stirred in the tent, not Silvanus, nor Constantine's armor-bearer. But the flap of the tent eased open, and in walked a man Constantine had never seen before. His gait was steady, his countenance regal, his eyes sparkled with warmth, and his wrists bore wounds the likes of which Constantine had never seen on a living soul.

The man stood in the middle of the tent and beckoned Constantine to stand. Constantine obeyed. Without knowing why, he dropped his sword.

"Constantine," the figure spoke gently.

"You know my name?" Constantine replied, chilled to the bone, his heart thumping.

"I think you will find," the man said, "that I know all names."

Constantine looked at Silvanus and his armor-bearer, both snoring loudly. Neither one was aware of this. He turned back to his visitor.

"Do I know you, sir?"

The man smiled. "I think what matters is that I know you, Constantine. And I know what you are now, but I know what you shall become, if you receive the sign."

It dawned on Constantine what this meant. "The sign? My lord, do you mean the cross in the sky?"

He blinked. The figure was gone. What was not missing, however, was the sense of peace that ruled Constantine's heart. And he remembered the message from the cross, as if his mysterious visitor was whispering it now.

"In this sign, you conquer."

It had taken only a word from Constantine for all the generals to assemble at two hours past midnight. Silvanus, Marcus, and Laurentius gathered around the table in the middle of the tent. Servants had laid a colored rug upon the table and the pegs and blocks representing the placement of cavalry, cohorts, light infantry, and reserves were arrayed before the senior staff. What surprised Marcus and Laurentius, however, was the placement of enemy representations on the field. What surprised Silvanus, as well, was the energy and peace in Constantine's dancing eyes.

"Silvanus has told you," Constantine began, "that as strange as it sounds, Maxentius has been moving his troops out of Rome and thrown aside all hope of waiting out a siege. This is not what we expected, but at least we know this ends later today."

"And you are certain, Silvanus, that Aelius and Celsus saw correctly?" asked Marcus.

"I trust them wholeheartedly, general," replied Silvanus. "They are our best spies."

"They also report another oddity," continued Constantine, "that Maxentius and his troops crossed to this side of the Tiber at midnight, having placed a large wooden bridge for transport across the waters. They must have had considerable portions of it built beforehand for ready assembly; you recall Maxentius had partially demolished the Milvian Bridge in case of a siege. This means they intend to bring the battle to us, although there are two other matters for concern, one for us, and one for Maxentius."

"Which are?" asked Laurentius.

Constantine pressed his fingertips upon the table-top before going on. "Aelius and Celsus also heard chatter from Maxentius' troops about 'both sections'. Celsus crept close enough to hear clanking of iron. It seems they are using fasteners for the bridge sections. If they must retreat, they will need the bridge, but if we pursue them, there is every reason to believe they might sabotage it to collapse under us."

"Or have archers with flaming arrows at the ready to burn it as we cross," averred Marcus, who tended to consider what else could go wrong with an attack.

"Regardless," Constantine spoke, his energy overcoming any lack of sleep, "this could turn to our tactical advantage. If Maxentius has come to our side of the river, he has little room to maneuver behind him, or to regroup if we push them back. I don't know why he has done this, other than the prophecy of a sacrifice by an augur, but there it is."

"The gods be thanked," Silvanus said, "for this is good fortune."

Constantine leaned on the table, framing his next words carefully. He knew no one would expect them.

"There is one other matter of preparation," he began, "and it comes from a vision I had earlier tonight. I want an emblem painted on the shields of every man of ours who holds one."

"At this late moment, that is unusual," said Laurentius, "but what does my lord desire?"

"I want a cross upon the shield of all soldiers in our legion," Constantine said firmly. "And I desire this symbol to be overlaid on it." He quickly sketched what looked like a P and an X, interlocking.

"What?" the three generals cried in surprise.

Marcus growled, "A cross and what looks like Greek lettering for Chi and Ro?"

"Yes, this," Constantine replied, holding a hand up to stay their protests. "And let me explain why." He proceeded to tell them about the cross and Chi-Ro in the evening sun and his perplexing encounter with his visitor during the night.

"The cross," Marcus finally spluttered. "Our execution device? More than that, the symbol of that crazed sect known as Christians! You would place that on our soldiers' means of protection?"

Laurentius shook his head. "I am all for whatever might secure victory, my lord, and I would not be as direct as Marcus, but your decision does make me wonder."

Silvanus straightened to his full height. "My lord," he said, "I am not doubting you believe what you saw and experienced, but strategically, this makes no sense. To give any credence to the Christians will confuse our legion, whose primary allegiance is to the gods. It seems capricious."

"And in our time together, good Silvanus," Constantine replied, his hands balling into fists, "have you ever known me to be impulsive or opportunistic? And if I truly am trying to seek a stratagem here, where does it lie? I know we are battling for Rome, center of the gods of old. I know many of our supporters behind that wall, those mistreated by Maxentius, worship the old gods."

"For that matter," Laurentius said, "I doubt the Christians have asked for your support, nor can you count on them for much yourself. They have become an increasingly pacifistic lot and few of them are within your army."

"And they are quite poor, as a general rule," Marcus reminded him. "Thus, if it is financial contribution you seek, you will be found lacking."

"All the more that you see reason, my generals!" Constantine shouted pounding the table with both fists. "To your eyes, none of this makes sense. You know I am not a man given to chance! I tell you I experienced what I did. Why can't my orders now be reasonable? And if the old gods are truly our guiding stars, then is it not possible they have brought Maxentius out here into open battle before us in such stupid fashion?"

Silvanus said nothing, tapping his fingers against the sheath of his sword, when he suddenly proclaimed, "I do not pretend to understand what you have said, Emperor Constantine, but I do believe that you have received a word for a new day."

"You say you believe what the Emperor believes?" barked the incredulous Marcus.

"I am saying I trust my Lord, yes," Silvanus declared.

"And I will say something that I am sure you know," Constantine replied. "These Christians have survived for years, when emperors past have sought to obliterate them, and their numbers have grown alongside their kindness and charity. So then there may be a power greater and more good than all else we have ever known. And if that God is calling me to obey Him now, I dare not go against Him."

Silvanus nodded. "I will give the order to bedeck the shields by your command, my lord."

"Good," Constantine smiled. "We move at daybreak.

The battle progressed better than even Constantine imagined. With swift attacks, his cavalry plunged into Maxentius' horsemen, flanking them at the edges and sending them toward the light infantry. Constantine trotted on his horse to a better vantage point and was pleased.

"They have nowhere to go," he pointed, turning to Silvanus. "The river is to their backs and the infantry and reserves are bunched in the middle."

"They will not last for more than a few minutes," Silvanus agreed as Marcus and Laurentius cried out, spurring the first five cohorts onward into the mass of Maxentius' troops. Suddenly, the sound of a horn pierced the air, and men wailed and shrieked as they turned toward the Tiber.

"They are headed for the bridge, my Lord!" Silvanus exclaimed. "They sounded the general retreat! I believed we would have victory, but to receive it this early, this decisively...it's..."

Constantine turned to him and smiled. "The work of God?"

Silvanus said nothing, shaking his head, stupefied, before noticing something else. "It's Maxentius on his horse! He's trying to make it back across the bridge."

"Well, let's not allow our troops to have all the fun!" Constantine yelled, urging his horse onward toward the battle. However, they were not needed. Even from a distance, Constantine could see the swarm of men pile on to the wooden bridge around Maxentius. Suddenly, the frightened horse of the enemy emperor reared back, and Maxentius flew from the saddle, bounced off a burly fellow in full retreat, and fell into the river. Constantine looked at the spot where he splashed into the waters, looking for a sign of his reappearance, when he realized it would not happen.

Worthy foe, Maxentius, he mused, but your armor has been your undoing and drowned you under those cold waves.

With the demise of their leader, Maxentius' troops fought briefly but with decreasing vigor. Finally, after about an hour, Constantine's troops surrounded them and claimed the victory. A shout went up, hailing Constantine as the undisputed emperor, and several soldiers broke out in song.

Silvanus, Marcus, and Laurentius approached Constantine, bowing as one before him. "Our unconquerable victor," Silvanus uttered. "We give thanks to you for this victory."

Surprising his generals, Constantine threw down his sword and knelt with them. "If you will allow me, I believe we must offer prayer and thanks to Another. It is I who give thanks to the Unconquerable Victor, Jesus Christ, for the victory this day truly belongs to Him."

CONSTANTINE's victory over the rebel emperor Maxentius secured his reign over the Western half of the Roman Empire, and within a few years, he extended his rule over the entire Empire from Britain to the Middle

East. An imperfect but sincere Christian, Constantine's reign marked the end of persecution against the Church, and he signed the Edict of Milan in 313, which named Christianity as an official and protected religion with the Roman Empire and restored property and rights to Christians who had been victims of persecution. Mindful of the potential for the Church to bring unity to his Empire, Constantine presided at the Council of Nicea (covered in the next chapter).

ATHANASIUS

June 325, Nicea

The stout, dark-skinned scholar wobbled to his seat in the imperial hall. The temperature outdoors in Nicea had dropped by ten degrees since yesterday, but the fresh air had yet to blow into the debate that had raged around him over the past month. Taking a seat on a bench on the south side of the council chamber, Athanasius watched his new friends Hosius, Macarius, and John talking in hushed tones near the throne from which the Emperor Constantine had opened the council just one month before. Hosius nodded in Athanasius' direction, beckoning him to draw near. Why do they need me? he wondered. Here they are, bishops from Cordova, Jerusalem, and Persia. Why do they require my voice? He fought the urge to close his eyes as he walked toward them, for he had slept perhaps two hours a night for the past week.

"Athanasius," Macarius smiled as he drew abreast of him, "we know you are tired, but as others are starting to trickle back into the hall, Hosius, John, and I wanted to speak with you privately. What happens next will be critical for our hopes."

"What do you mean?" Athanasius rasped. "We have been speaking over one another's heads for the past few days. The only reason I am here is because Bishop Alexander is too frail for the journey and I am here as his bishop-designate. I know we have some critical steps that follow, but why do you need to make that especially clear to me?"

Hosius looked around the hall, more bishops streaming in. It seemed that in no time all three hundred representatives would fill the chamber once more. Leaning toward Athanasius, Hosius spread his hands with palms down, as if the motion would quell Athanasius' queries. "It's just this, Athanasius: We have spoken at great length over many details. Arius' followers are fewer than we are, but more vocal. As churchmen, we know how we might manage the chaos that follows, but we cannot do this alone. This is where we must lean on you."

"On me?" Athanasius was incredulous.

John of Persia nodded, reaching down from his towering height and placing a stocky-hand on Athanasius' neck. "Yes, my friend. You. You have been at the center of this storm since it broke in Alexandria. You preached and proclaimed against the errors that Arius continues to spout regarding our eternal Lord Jesus!"

"I did that in the churches, in worship!" Athanasius protested. "To ordinary people, so they could grasp and eat the simple food of God's truth. You are asking something else of me now, to make lofty arguments before all the learned bishops of the Church around the world!"

"That is exactly what we are doing, Athanasius," Hosius interrupted, raising a finger to stop Athanasius' emerging protest. "Eusebius of Nicomedia has been marshaling an impressive tally from Scripture designed to prove Arius' views. The days of you sitting politely by and agreeing alongside us are over! This is the day you were born for, the day to lead us. This next session will be about the nature of our Lord from the Holy Scriptures!" He pressed two fingers into Athanasius' chest. "And you know your theology! And our Savior will not be honored if you cannot make your stand!"

Athanasius peered around the hall. Nearly every bishop had returned, and the volume of noise had increased throughout the hall. Turning back to the three bishops, Athanasius nodded. "As God wills, I will do."

"And we will be with you, good servant," Macarius bowed to him.

Why, oh why am I pressed on all sides now? Athanasius asked himself. He thought back to the day before he left, when his bishop Alexander warned him of the days to come. For years, they had stood against Arius' catchy poems and eloquent sermons, in which the presbyter had decried any sense of Jesus' eternal nature. Jesus had to have a beginning, Arius proclaimed, because if He is the Son of God, He cannot be equal to the Father. If Christ and God were equal, Jesus would be God's Brother, not His Son! The only conclusion we can draw, Arius called forth daringly, is that Jesus was the first created being, neither fully God nor mere man, but something in between. And how often Arius danced at the head of prancing columns of humanity roaming through the streets of Alexandria, singing,

"O Jesus, great one God hath brought,
the one who joined our human lot,
of Him hear what the truth hath wrought:
There was a time when He was not!"[1]

Nothing made Athanasius shake with holy rage like those sneering hymns, and Athanasius remembered how, on that day, it had taken Alexander much time, and several goblets of wine, to calm his young deacon.

"I do not understand Bishop Alexander, and I would never go against your order given my vow of obedience, but how can you expect me to be of much good at Nicea?"

Alexander had nodded his aged head. "You might not believe that many will listen, but I have been attending

1. Based on Arius' theology and the fact he was known to compose songs to make his beliefs more "catchy" to others. https://www.johnsanidopoulos.com/2011/06/poisonous-songs-of-arius.html

to your wisdom for some time, and it is insight beyond your tender years. That is why I have made you, deacon though you are, my successor. And do not be surprised when other bishops recognize your wisdom and seek you out, not merely to speak, but to lead. Remember the story of Mordecai, my son."

Athanasius had shifted his feet, knowing where this was leading. "Esther's cousin?"

"Yes. He told her, 'How do you not know that you have been raised up for such a time as this?'"

For such a time as this, for such a time as this, for such... Suddenly, Athanasius was brought back to reality. His friend Nicholas, the bishop of Myra, stormed across the floor. Several of the Arian supporters screamed at him, and his face was red as raw meat. Depositing himself on the bench next to Athanasius in the rapidly crowding hall, Nicholas sent a blast of angry air through his nostrils.

"What happened?" Athanasius pleaded with him.

"Arius!" Nicholas huffed. "Trying to worm his way in here when he isn't supposed to be since he's only a presbyter! I called out the cheater in front of his friends and he started singing one of his annoying hymns. So I did the only thing I could!"

"Which was what?"

"I punched him!" Nicholas replied, bug-eyed and arms spread wide. "I wasn't going to let him get away with his heresy. Is that what you want?"

"I want none of it, Nicholas, but that includes you losing your temper!" Athanasius scolded him. "Do you really think that will help our cause? Is that really who you are supposed to be? You're known for relieving the poor, for taking gifts around Myra to the children in time of need! You're not a brawler! Can't you let God's truth do the fighting?"

"Then you'd better tie me to this bench before I forget myself again," Nicholas growled.

"Let's quiet ourselves. Hosius is calling the speakers forth."

It took Eusebius of Nicomedia some time to read from his page. His notes were flawless, his voice melodious, and he possessed such a high volume of Scripture that the followers of Arius nodded and cheered passionately, believing their case to be won beyond reasonable doubt.

"We know that we all should appeal to the Scriptures," Eusebius purred, giving Hosius a hard look and then Constantine's legate a more jovial gaze. "None of our opponents would doubt the place of Proverbs within the canon, where it speaks of God's work at creation and says, 'The LORD created me at the beginning of His work.' Now, I ask you all, good bishops and representatives, is not the beginning of the Almighty's work the event of creation itself? And if the speaker was created then, who else could be speaking but Jesus, years before He walked this earth, but referring to a specific beginning. Yes, good men, there was a time when He was not.

"And what about the very words of Luke the Evangelist, when he records that Jesus grew in wisdom and stature, and in favor with God and with man? Is this not evidence that if Jesus grew, He must have grown from a fixed event, a starting point, a genesis of existence? Can we ignore the words of Jesus himself, according to the apostle John, when the Christ said 'The Father is greater than I?'"

The stirring tone whipped the hall into a frenzy, the Arians cheering at full voice and Hosius and his side raising angry denouncements. Eusebius looked around the chamber, soaking in what he had provoked. Athanasius did not believe for a moment that Arius' friend regretted it; in fact, he seemed to be savoring the moment entirely.

"Finally, good bishops, not only do we have evidence from the Hebrew Scriptures, from Luke's Gospel, and from the admittance of Jesus himself, but we hear the words of the apostle Paul who declares to the believers at Colosse that Christ is the firstborn...I repeat, the firstborn over all creation! Yes, my fellow bishops, be there no doubt from Holy Scripture that there was a time when Jesus was not! Eternal He never was!"

The hall was now a cauldron of noise. A storm on the Mediterranean Sea would scarcely have drowned out the strident calls from both sides. Hosius approached Eusebius and his allies, frowning and making angry gestures, when suddenly the eyes of each man in the chamber turned and looked at the person who had swept to the center of the imperial hall. Every eye was fixed on Athanasius.

"My good Hosius," he declared, astonishing himself with his boldness, "I ask an opportunity to counter the good bishop Eusebius."

"You!" sneered a bishop in the northwest corner. "Looks like you've spent more time in the sun than with your books!"

"Let's see if your arguments can outlast your height, little man!" chortled another.

"Ho, everyone, silence for the Black Dwarf!" came a further slur.

Hosius, Macarius, John, and Nicholas leapt from their seats to answer the attacks, Nicholas with his fists bunched tightly for another fight. But Athanasius interposed himself between his friends and the opposing side, wheeling on the Arians with sudden vigor.

"I had no idea that the purpose of this council was to find anything other than the truth!" he shouted. "You," he pointed to those who had belittled him, "who see fit to deride and discredit me because of my stature or skin, who declare me a dark stump of a man and no better than a proconsul's jester, as you have cheered your speaker's use of Scripture, you will most certainly listen to mine and the logic that follows!"

The thunder that bolted from Athanasius' mouth quieted the hall in an instant. No one moved, and all listened as the young man spread his arms wide.

"No doubt you have appealed to Scripture, good bishops, but you skimmed the ocean waves while failing to plunge into the depths of the sea to observe what dwells there! You appeal to Proverbs, failing to admit that the speaker is the personification of Wisdom itself. Eusebius and all with him, you dare to place Christ in the breach because you wish Him to be the created one rather than eternal. I say to you that the Scriptures must shape your observation of them, not the reverse fashion!

"You speak of Luke's record of the Savior's growth. Of course, He would grow. As fully human, He must. And as fully human, He would represent us and take our sin. But does that deny the eternal nature of Christ, or does it adorn it with beauty? Can Jesus not claim the Father was greater than He, the Son? He submitted to the Father's will, of course. but does this make Him any less divine, any less eternal, any less God?

"And you, Eusebius, who uproot the treasure of Colossians and speak of Christ as the firstborn of all creation. Why do you use that word as if to speak of our Lord having a beginning, when it is clear to the lowliest scholar of the text that 'firstborn' can mean 'ruler', as well? What do you do with the words placed only lines after your text of choice, which clearly say of our Lord Jesus that in Him all the fullness of God was pleased to dwell? All the fullness? And you claim there was a time when Jesus was not?

"Shall we ignore the clear testimony of the apostle John when he begins his Gospel speaking of Jesus as the Word...in the beginning was the Word, and the Word was with God, and the Word was God! He was, is, and always will be eternal God! How can your lot deny that from

Scripture? Do you dare deny the words to the Hebrews where the Father declares to the Son, 'your throne, O God, is established forever?' Is God a liar, good bishops? Is the apostle Paul, when he reminds Titus that we are waiting for our blessed hope, the appearing of the glory of our great God and Savior, Jesus Christ?"

Athanasius pointed to the crowd, rotating around to make sure all received his words clearly. "You cannot have this in divided fashion! You cannot worship Christ and deny His eternal nature! You cannot place Him among us and deny His Godhood! He is before all time, the Creator of time who dwelt in time amongst us who are marked by time! Nothing can deliver us from sin and death and hell but an eternal Jesus, fully human and fully divine, eternal and of one substance with the Father! And on this truth, there can be no compromise!"

Cheers erupted throughout the hall. Even some of the quieter and more diffident Arians stood and applauded. Eusebius shot up from his bench and tried to wave away the roars, even as he saw he must think quickly of a way to stem the tide.

"Order, order! Hosius, quiet your supporters!"

"We will silence ourselves," Hosius replied, "when we have come to an agreement."

"If it's an agreement you desire," Eusebius growled back, "then we must find one that pleases us all."

"We must agree to the truth, good Eusebius!" Athanasius announced, bringing another round of cheers. "And as you have struggled to make it clear, perhaps we should fashion the statement of which you speak."

Macarius, who had drawn beside them, clapped Eusebius on the shoulder as the cheers rent the air. "That seems like the best idea I've heard since we arrived in Nicea." He, Hosius, and John pulled Athanasius back to the bench, where Nicholas nearly crushed him with a tremendous hug.

"Well done, my friend," he wept, "and thank you for undoing my impetuousness."

Athanasius clasped Nicholas' arm, his own eyes shining when Hosius approached and clasped his other arm. "I told you, Athanasius, you know your theology. And you made your stand."

He paused, then said, "I have to say, I am sure our Savior was pleased with you this day."

ATHANASIUS served as a deacon in the great city of Alexandria, Egypt, caring for the Christians there and preaching faithfully. His biblical teaching drew the opposition of Arius, who taught that Jesus was not eternal and was not truly God. The long-standing argument, known as the Arian Controversy, was so severe it threatened to split Constantine's newly-won Empire, and so the emperor called for a great council at Nicea from May to August 325. There, Athanasius' impassioned use of Scripture and careful presentation of the biblical evidence for Jesus' nature turned a contentious debate toward a functional consensus that Jesus was the eternal Son of God, "begotten, not made, of one substance with the Father." The resulting accord written by the bishops at this council is what we know as the Nicene Creed. Athanasius succeeded Alexander as bishop of Alexandria in 328. Even after his work at Nicea, Athanasius suffered much, facing exile many times when local Arian rulers or later emperors wanted him banished. But he never turned aside from proclaiming the glory of the eternal Son of God and salvation in the person and work of Jesus Christ.

FACT FILES

The Conversion of Armenia

On occasion, people attempt to demonstrate the important role religion has played in the development of nations. In my own country, the United States, we can trace many of our roots to English Pilgrims who came to America for religious freedom. Many nations still retain official state religions, even if all faiths receive freedom of worship. For example, the Church of England remains the state church of (naturally) England. The Scandinavian nations like Denmark, Norway, and Sweden are officially Lutheran nations. Greece recognizes the Orthodox Church as its official church, and small nations like Liechtenstein and Malta have declared the Catholic Church as their national faith.

This is not to say that religion runs the government in these countries (that can bring its own problems!) or that everyone in these nations belongs to those official churches. But the close relationship between religion and government has been a factor for many years, and the secularism that marks a number of places in the world is a relatively new development in the history of mankind.

For many years after Jesus' ascension into heaven, the Christian Church did not prioritize influence or national leadership. Most Christians were just trying to survive and weather the storms of persecution. But in the years before Constantine would grant many freedoms to Christianity throughout the Roman Empire, the diligent ministry of one man caused an entire nation to call itself Christian. That nation was Armenia.

Armenia was located between Asia Minor (now Turkey) and the region of Persia (now Iran) and it was a long-standing battleground for many years between Rome and

Persia. While Roman religion honored gods like Jupiter, Juno, Mars, and Pluto, and while Christianity proclaimed salvation through Jesus Christ alone, Armenia developed its own mythology; its pantheon included the chief god Aramazd and the fertility goddess Astghik, among others. Later, a Persian-based religion known as Zoroastrianism—which emphasized the eternal struggle between equally strong forces of good and evil—became the primary religion of the region well into the third century A.D., when an unlikely hero arose within the land.

His name was Grigor Lusavorich, better known as Gregory the Illuminator. Born into a noble family in Armenia, his youth was marked by controversy and catastrophe. Gregory's father Anak was accused of assassinating King Khosrov II of Armenia; he was swiftly executed, and the royal family sought out the rest of Gregory's household. A couple, Sopia and Yevtagh, took him with them and escaped to Cappadocia. There, a priest named Euthalius educated Gregory and taught him the Scriptures, leading Gregory to embrace the Gospel of Jesus Christ.

It was several years later, when Gregory was about thirty years old, that he was seized with a passion to return to his homeland of Armenia. Tradition maintained that the apostles Bartholomew and Thaddeus had preached Christ to the Armenians years before, but paganism now drenched the land. His people needed to hear of Jesus Christ, Gregory reasoned, but he was also motivated by another desire. Remembering his father's evil act in murdering the previous king, Gregory believed he could satisfy the guilt of that crime by evangelizing the nation of his birth.

In spite of Gregory's sincerity, he was returning to Armenia during the reign of Tiridates III, the son of the murdered Khosrov II. Knowing that Gregory was Anak's son, Tiridates first ordered Gregory to offer sacrifice to a Zoroastrian goddess. When Gregory refused, the king furiously commanded that Gregory be thrown into and kept in a dungeon for a dozen years near Ararat (interestingly enough, the region where Noah's ark came to rest after the flood waters receded!). Like Joseph in the Old Testament, Gregory was wrongly imprisoned and had to wait out his days with patience.

It was here that national circumstances intervened, as Tiridates, abandoned by the Roman emperor Diocletian, found the pressure of ruling a nation under attack from Persia too taxing. His health and his mind began to slip, and he began to exhibit wildly feral behavior, like an animal. Tiridates' sister, Khosrovidukht, in a moment of sheer desperation, inquired at the dungeon in Ararat and found Gregory there, thin, starving, but still very much alive. Believing this to be a miracle, Khosrovidukht begged Gregory to perform one of his own by healing her brother the king. The prisoner and the monarch met, and Gregory's prayers and pleadings had a powerful effect on Tiridates. Before long, he had restored the king to full health in body and mind. Overwhelmed by Gregory's healing power, Tiridates forsook the old religion and immediately proclaimed that Armenia would worship the Lord Jesus Christ, appointing Gregory as the head of the new Armenian church.

The conversion of Armenia did not mean that everyone within its regions became sincere Christian believers. Gregory still had to labor diligently to evangelize portions of Armenia with the Gospel. But his work in healing and converting King Tiridates III gave Christianity a foothold within a rugged, pagan nation before Constantine would provide freedom and relief for Christianity throughout the Roman Empire. And the Armenian Apostolic Church continues to this day in spite of great persecution, inflicted by Persia at different times throughout history, and suffering greatly when Turkey systematically murdered over a million ethnic Armenians from 1914 to 1923. Such endurance follows well from the legacy of Gregory the Illuminator, whose dream to Christianize his homeland was fulfilled by God's mercy in remarkable ways.

AMBROSE

386, Milan

The crowds that swarmed the city streets had swelled within the last week. *Once again, the worshipers of Christ would celebrate the resurrection of their Lord,* Ambrose thought, the true heartbeat of the Gospel. All the weariness of his duties seemed to melt away in light of the coming solemn yet merry services. Ambrose was busier than he could ever remember. He was circuiting the city and surrounding region, encouraging the priests at the local churches and imploring them to preach the eternal Christ from His Word. He had trouble sleeping, yet he used these restless times to pen chants and hymns that his churches could use in public worship throughout the year. He was inwardly rehearsing his sermon for this Easter Sunday, even as he remembered the need to prepare for Monday's session with his students and protégés. They would be discussing Plato, the fine points of rhetoric, and the parables of Christ. Ambrose grinned in anticipation, for his prize student, Augustine, was beginning to show a great deal of raw energy and passion for his new-found faith. Ambrose wondered where the Holy Spirit would be leading that young man in the future.

His thoughts were interrupted by a clattering of feet against the steps of the church. Looking up, Ambrose saw two soldiers running toward him, the late-afternoon sun shining off their helmets. He knew both of them, so he instinctively realized they did not approach to arrest him.

But their anxious looks did not set well with Ambrose, and a knot began to form in his stomach.

"Your Grace!" the older of the two called as they drew near. Ambrose raised his hand to acknowledge their presence.

"Blasius, Otho," he replied. "Normally, I wouldn't expect to see the two of you out and about on Holy Saturday[1]. I was headed to the church to pray. But I assume what you have to tell me is quite important."

"We can make it brief and plain," Blasius nodded, "but we require speed and craft. Where shall we go?"

Ambrose indicated toward the church. "In the Portiana, gentlemen. Let us..." His voice trailed off, and looking back he was certain for a moment that he saw the flash of a purple robe vanish down a side street. He waggled his head, then turned back to the men. "Let us go and we can speak inside."

"We are sorry to interrupt your preparation, Your Grace," spoke Otho, whose face looked so young and smooth Ambrose could scarcely imagine he'd begun to shave. "However, recent developments demand this warning."

"I imagine," Ambrose said quietly, by the light of a recently-ignited candle, "this has to do with the emperor's mother?"

"Justina truly has spies everywhere, Ambrose," Blasius replied in his throaty, gravelly voice, "but this goes even beyond her past capabilities."

"And we know you need people you can trust, Your Grace," added Otho.

Ambrose smiled and patted Otho's shoulder. "Good Otho, your mother has long been an honest and godly woman, and she was one of my brightest students to come for baptism. If you are half the person she is, I have no

1. The day before Easter Sunday on the church calendar.

doubt of your trustworthiness. And I have always relied on Blasius' word, as well."

"All of which is good," acknowledged Blasius, "because we require speed to bludgeon this insidious threat."

"Justina has not been happy with me for some time," Ambrose said knowingly, "although my thrift and provision for others are hardly worthy of her venom. I know that she loves her son very much, and she wishes to make an example of me during the Easter service tomorrow, does she not?"

"It is both more complex and more horrible than that," Blasius grumbled. "Ever since your friend Emperor Gratian was killed, Justina has steered her dear Valentinian deeper and deeper into Arian ground.

"Be that as it may," Blasius continued, "there is a more imminent threat."

"How imminent?" asked Ambrose.

"Tomorrow," Otho blurted out.

"Tomorrow?" Ambrose replied. "Easter Sunday? When we are worshiping the risen Lord?"

"If Justina and Valentinian have their way, you will never have opportunity to see that altar for the Eucharist, Your Grace," Blasius hissed. "She is secretly planning to enter the nave[2] and claim this cathedral as an Arian house of worship!"

Ambrose went silent. All his preparation, his study, his endeavors. Nothing could have prepared him for this horrid news. The emperor and his mother seeking to claim the Lord's house for their twisted doctrine!

"You see why we had to tell you, Your Grace," Blasius' words cut through the bishop's thoughts.

"How shall you respond, good Ambrose?" Otho asked.

Ambrose looked at both men. "Through my time in Milan, the speed of my life has been too brisk. I have

2. The main part of the church building.

worried that things happened too quickly. I was a lawyer, a governor, only fourteen years ago. All I did was come to this church to prevent the uproar during the election of the next bishop after the death of the other."

"I remember that day," Blasius said admiringly.

"Yes, you kept the crowd at bay," Ambrose replied wistfully, "I do not know what stirred the crowd to a fever pitch, but they called for me to take the bishop's staff instead. I wasn't a churchman! I was a lawyer!"

"Not for long," recalled Blasius.

"No, and everything happened so fast. After all, no honest person, myself included, could say I was prepared for that. So, I refused it. I was neither trained in theology, nor had I even been baptized! The crowd was pressing upon me to accept what I could not do."

"So what did you do?" Otho asked.

"I fled," Ambrose replied, rubbing his hands and shuffling his feet. "I went to my friend Salvius' home. I stayed there half a month, but Emperor Gratian intervened in the only way he knew how. He told me I could refuse his offer, but he added that others fully accepted me and judged me worthy of being a bishop. I still might have refused if Salvius hadn't told Gratian where I was. I said I would consider Gratian's offer if I was properly trained first. Within a week I was baptized, made deacon, then priest, then bishop of this city."

"Thus, you know something of the need to act quickly," Blasius uttered.

"That's only because there were faithful people who were able to train me in the Scriptures," Ambrose sighed in reply. "And now with Valentinian and Justina acting in concert with Auxentius, it appears the Christian Gospel found in Holy Scripture is under attack. They mean to take this church."

"They do," Blasius replied.

"Will you concede?" Otho asked.

"The very idea is outrageous!" Ambrose exclaimed. "There are those who would argue to concede today to fight later, that we can give up a place and meet elsewhere, for the Gospel extends beyond walls and mortar. Well, I shall not listen to them! I will not give the ground of this basilica to anyone, because I am Milan's bishop, and the sheep of this city are entrusted to my tender and devoted care! If they will take this church, it will be to pull that staff out of my cold, dead fingers!"

Blasius smiled, loving the fire he saw in the bishop's eyes. He stood at attention. "And what does my bishop command?"

The first rays of the sun poked through the windows of the Basilica Portiana the next morning. Thousands of celebrating, yet anxious, souls stood within the nave of the church as Blasius ordered soldiers to ring around the periphery of the interior. Cries from the street erupted from time to time, but many of the worshipers inside paid little heed to such noises, preferring instead to quietly greet each other with an earnest "Christ is risen" then respond with, "He is risen indeed!"

Finally, shouts rang from the outside, growing closer. With worried looks, the assembly turned back toward the entry doors, expecting them to open allowing the emperor, his mother, and their guards to spill inside.

Instead, what they saw was Ambrose, their bishop, go to the doors, lift a beam in his arms, and slam it upon the iron handles, securing it shut. The clang of the wood against iron reverberated throughout the nave, and Ambrose turned to the congregation.

"We worship the Triune God, not the praise of man!" he shouted.

"Do you worship the Triune God, my fellow Christians?" Ambrose called again.

"We do!" The assembly shouted as one.

"Do you bow before the throne of Christ, or the swords of the emperor?" he asked them.

"The throne of Christ! The throne of Christ! The throne of Christ!" the worshipers roared together.

"And who is King over all?" Ambrose asked aloud, his voice filling the nave with power and authority. "Is it the risen eternal Son of God, our Lord Jesus Christ? Or is it the Emperor Valentinian? Or his mother who lurks in the shadows? I ask you, who is King over all?"

"The Son of God! The Son of God! The Son of God!" All called out together with reverent vigor.

"Is the grave inhabited or broken? Is it sealed or smashed?"

"The grave is empty!" shouted Marcus, the deacon.

"We worship the Lord who defeated death!" called forth a woman near the front of the nave.

Ambrose smiled broadly and raised his hands, standing in the center aisle of the nave.

"Christ is risen!" he sang.

"He is risen indeed!" came the reply.

"Christ is risen!"

"He is risen indeed!"

"Christ is risen!"

"He is risen indeed!" came the final response.

And at that moment, a booming sound came from the entry doors.

The doors creaked, but held firm. Whatever the soldiers used as a battering ram, it swayed the doors, but the frame did not break. For several minutes, the pounding rhythm continued, but Ambrose held firm in the middle aisle. When it became clear the smashing would not cease, and equally clear that the worshipers were growing more anxious, Ambrose spread his arms wide and began to sing.

"The morning kindles all the sky,
the heavens resound with anthems high,
The shining angels as they speed,
proclaim 'The Lord is risen indeed!'"[3]

Softly at first, and then with increasing strength, others began to join in.

"Vainly with rocks His tomb was barred
while Roman guards kept watch and ward.
Majestic from the spoiled tomb,
In pomp of triumph, He has come!"

The pounding at the doors continued. It did not matter. Now the lilting chorus became a roaring tumult.

"When the amazed disciples heard,
their hearts with speechless joy were stirred;
their Lord's beloved face to see,
Eager they haste with hearts so free.
His pierced hands to them He shows,
His face with love's own radiance glows.
They with the angels' message speed,
And shout, 'The Lord is risen indeed!'"

Ambrose lifted his eyes to heaven as they lifted the final verse to heaven.

"O Christ, Thou King compassionate!
Our hearts possess, on Thee we wait:
Help us to render praises due,
To Thee the endless ages through!"

3. The entire hymn can be found at https://hymnary.org/text/the_morning_kindles_all_the_sky_the_heav

With the final notes falling from their lips, a crashing sound brought the hymn to a sudden halt. Striding in from the southwest corner of the nave, the empress mother Justina herself bolted toward Ambrose with flames in her bright green eyes. A hush fell over the congregation, many of them bowing out of habit. However, as Justina scurried up the center aisle, Ambrose stood unmoving.

"The raining of glass from behind us," he said gently, "betrays your manner of entry, O Justina."

"This is the result of your madness, you Athanasian brute!" Justina yelled, specks of saliva flying from her mouth. "I am here as your sovereign to demand your expulsion from this place, which is to be hallowed as a place of worship to the true God of heaven!"

"I believe that," Ambrose calmly replied, "it already is."

"We have been over this ground before, bishop..."

"And if you bring your Arian grovelers here," Ambrose said, with a trace of a growl in his voice, "it will cease to be a portal to heaven. Deny the eternal Son of God, deny the Lord God Himself!"

"Ambrose, I have warned you long enough!"

"Yes, you have. I find it interesting it is you doing the warning and not your son, the emperor."

"He speaks the truth!" called out a congregant from the front.

"Ambrose! Ambrose! Ambrose!" chanted the crowd over and over.

"Silence!" yelled Justina.

"Ambrose! Ambrose! Ambrose!"

"Quiet yourselves!" "Ambrose! Ambrose! Ambrose! Ambrose! Ambrose!"

Furious, Justina wheeled on Ambrose. "You deny my orders, you pig! If you want to keep your church, you will do so at a price! If you will not give up this nave to Arian glory, then you must take the sacred vases of worship and deliver them to my son the emperor."

The assembly quieted, straining to hear Ambrose's reply. They wanted to remain with him. Would he bow to give the empress an honorable retreat?

She stepped to within six inches of him. "Ambrose, when the Goths invaded soon after your consecration and demanded ransom for the captives from our city, you melted the golden vessels and ornaments of this very church and gave the new coinage to their king. You defended your decision by saying It is better to preserve for the Lord souls rather than gold. It is better to keep the living vessels, than the golden ones."

She looked up in his face, sneering with undisguised venom. "Thus, the price for this church to remain as yours will be the gold it possesses."

Ambrose released a sigh from his mouth and, looking around his church at those gathered, shook his head vigorously. And then he took his index finger and pointed it straight between Justina's eyes.

"No, Justina. It is not right for me to give up these things, nor for him to take them. So, go to your son, and admit to him that you both desire a blood price for this church more than the living God! And as for me and my house, we will serve the risen Lord!"

The symphony of joy that exploded from the crowd drowned out Justina's wails and shrieks. Turning on her heels, she fled from the Portiana in a fury. With smiles on their faces, the congregation broke into another song that Ambrose had taught them so well.

"O Jesus, Lord of heavenly grace,
Thou brightness of Thy Father's face,
Thou Fountain of eternal light
Whose beams disperse the shades of night.
O Christ, with each returning morn,
Thine image to our hearts is borne!

O may we ever clearly see our Savior
and our God in Thee!"[4]

AMBROSE served as the bishop of Milan from 374 to 397, overseeing the church during some of the most tumultuous times in ancient history. Losing his friend the emperor Gratian by assassination, Ambrose shepherded his churches in Milan with an unwavering devotion to the eternal Jesus Christ as he faithfully preached Nicene doctrine. His defiant stand in the Basilica Portiana on Easter Sunday in 386 was part of a series of courageous stands against the rulers and Arian usurpers of his day, a passion and faithfulness he would pass down to his most famous student, Augustine.

4. Penned by Ambrose. https://hymnary.org/text/o_jesus_lord_of_heavenly_grace

JOHN CHRYSOSTOM

401, Constantinople

The windy drafts from the Black Sea swept through the open window in the cathedral's study chamber. The preacher, his robe wrapped closely around him to defend against the chill of the gusts, leaned over his table, peering over the words in the book to his left and pressing the reed pen with his right hand into the small bowl of ink. Shaking the pen gently, he lightly inscribed the Greek letters in a patient, even hand, writing out the words he knew would once again shake the foundations of this, his beloved city.

Without warning the door flew open, and a guard, dressed smartly in the emperor's regalia, entered the room. Even the noise of his entry did not startle the preacher, who continued to write until he had finished the sentence he had begun. Placing the pen upon the table, he flexed his fingers and rubbed his hands, the aches within his joints warning him of his increasing age.

"Your Grace, the abbot of Sorbia has arrived," the guard announced.

The preacher turned, wincing from the aches in his hands, and shook his head as he sighed, "I've told you before that you do not need to call me that. Titles are unnecessary for the Lord's servants. Call me John."

"Your Grace, I decline," the guard replied, "due to the palace protocol to which I am sworn, although I note your objection. The abbot waits outside. Shall I send him in?"

"By all means," John smiled.

Into the room stepped a stocky man, nearly the preacher's age, with a salt-and-pepper beard hugging his craggy face. "My friend, Chrysostom!" he hailed, raising his hands and embracing John, who accepted his exuberance with a weary grin.

"Evagrius, my dear friend," John Chrysostom cried, waving him to a seat near the window.

"Shall I fetch a flagon of wine?" the soldier asked.

"No wine, my good man," Chrysostom replied, "for the richness of the liquid is not becoming to a meeting between ministers of the Gospel. But perhaps you could ask for some water to be brought to us? The sacristan, could fetch it," Chrysostom reminded him. "He is preparing the altar for the Eucharist tomorrow."

"With a good will, Your Grace," the guard uttered, falling back on his formality.

As the door closed, Evagrius' smile disappeared and he slumped in his chair. "My good friend, I received word last week of the trouble that is brewing in this city against you once again. The news flies over the breadth of the empire with speed greater than eagles. What is it that has Constantinople in an uproar?"

"You forget, my good Evagrius," Chrysostom began, "that our Lord Jesus told his followers that we would be hated. He said as the world hated Him, it will hate us. And the world has entered the church to attack us."

"I feared this would happen when you accepted this post, John," Evagrius grunted. "But I cannot see how you bear up under such weight! Theophilus barks from Alexandria that you are a heretic and give shelter to heretics. Your spurning of lavish dress and affluent living has made you popular with the masses and the enemy of the elite. Your preaching is pulled faithfully from the meat of Scripture itself and yet so many criticize it for lacking imagination. Just yesterday, I broke down and cried that our Church should be so fractured and forgetful less than a century after we united at Nicea."

Chrysostom looked thoughtful as the door opened again and the sacristan stood there with a tray, a pitcher, and two cups. "Your water, good bishop."

"Thank you, my son," Chrysostom replied, gesturing to a low table by the door. "Please leave it there."

Chrysostom then poured a cup of cool water for Evagrius, before continuing. "To this day, I cannot understand why Theophilus desires to bring me down. I have merely stated I believe Origen that God in His normal sense is spirit and not flesh. Of course, God became man in the person of Christ. No one disputes that! But Theophilus seeks to paint me with different colors. He is spreading lies that I believe God is spirit all the time at the expense of Jesus' humanity. And he aligns me with other teachings of Origen that I do not accept. But the lies have flown around the empire before the truth can adorn itself with a tunic."

"You know Theophilus' ambassador has arrived in the Empress Eudoxia's court today."

"Good Evagrius, if he has, then I place myself under the sovereign will of the Triune God. I will not be frightened into avoiding conflict. The Empress has so dominated her court that her weak-willed husband Arcadius will not raise a voice of protest. She expects me to attend court parties, the games, and festivals, and to dress the part of a wealthy noble. Am I a senator? Am I a king? No, I am a pastor, disgusted by how so many priests, deacons, and other bishops have fallen into the trappings of wealth and possessions. How can I preach the law of God's demands and the grace of Christ's abundant love and not ally myself with the poor as my Lord did?"

"You and I are becoming a rare breed, Chrysostom," Evagrius sighed, taking a sip of water. "We are compelled by the Holy Spirit to recall we are primarily shepherds, not kings."

"Which means we should expect all that comes with it, friend!" exclaimed Chrysostom. "I am not an emperor. I am not even a wealthy merchant sending goods throughout the trade routes that extend from this city. I am a pastor. My work is not to dine on roasted meat and guzzle the finest wine. My work is like that of a man cleaning a patch of filthy ground into which a muddy stream is constantly running. Others may disdain that, but if it is God's calling for us who are pastors, should that not be enough?"

The door flew open again, and into the room came a swaggering young man dressed in a red cowl with a gold cape. Tossing a jeweled walking stick ungraciously on the papers stacked upon Chrysostom's table, the intruder rubbed his chin and walked up to the bishop himself, eye to eye from inches away.

"You seem to have forgotten good manners, Ambassador Nicorious," Chrysostom spoke firmly, "and you have either forced your way past my sacristan or entered unknown. Either way, you are here unbidden."

"I am sent bidden by another," Nicorious bellowed in response, "Her Highness the Empress of the Empire has implored me to approach you and remind you that you serve by her good graces..."

"The good grace by which I serve comes from God," Chrysostom demurred.

"There you go again, bishop, deflecting the conversation from the danger that threatens to swallow you up. Why do you have to be so difficult? Why do you remove priests from our court and banish them from Constantinople?"

"I merely redirected them so they might perform their tasks to which they were called by God!" Chrysostom shouted back. "They are priests serving churches outside of this city. Their people starve waiting for the meat and milk of God's Holy Word, while these men parade and dance in royal splendor. So, I ordered them back, yes, because

God called them and I ordained them to tasks within their churches, not the castle of our empire!"

"Your actions on behalf of the commoners may gain you their loyalty," Nicorious sneered, "but the truth is your few friends at court have been disappearing. The Empress's chief counselor is no longer with us..."

"Conveniently so, as Eudoxia herself had him executed."

"And you expel bishops and anger priests with your insistence on simplicity. You insist on biting the hand that feeds you, Chrysostom. It would be wise that you use tomorrow to choose new waters in which to swim."

"What do you mean, Nicorious?" The question came from Evagrius, who could hold his tongue no longer.

"I mean that you pull back from your endeavors, and utilize tomorrow's sermon in the Eucharist to signal just that," Nicorious wagged a finger toward Chrysostom. "Pull back from your condemnations against extravagance and vice, and note that Jesus and his disciples never lacked for what they needed in food, drink, and shelter."

"Never lacking," Chrysostom replied, with a glint of anger in his eyes, "is different from opulence!"

"And you, will affirm that the Empress's rule is, to us, as the rule of Christ, for the Lord orders us not to defy the one who bears the sword!"

Chrysostom crossed the room, opening the door and nodding for Nicorious to leave. "Tell her majesty that I will ascend the pulpit of the church tomorrow, and that I will most definitely preach God's Holy Word. But be assured that although I am aware the Empress' likeness is borne on coins throughout the Empire, my primary concern is whether her name is in the Lamb's Book of Life!"

Nicorious swept his cloak around him and, scowling, left the chamber. Chrysostom shut the door and leaned against it, groaning softly. Evagrius stood from his seat and bowed toward the bishop.

"John," he uttered, "I was going to ask how you will put the Word of God before His lambs tomorrow, but I think now I know what to expect."

He paused, then drew to Chrysostom's side. "And God will be with you, my friend."

The Megale Ekklesia—the Great Church of Constantinople—was full to overflowing the next morning. Empress Eudoxia sat in the elevated perch with her entourage, set into the far wall just above the level of Chrysostom's pulpit. Her husband Arcadius was nowhere to be seen, but she never allowed him to wield his power, especially within these walls. She turned to Nicorious. "Is everything settled? He is going to speak apologetically and place himself under royal mercy?"

"I outlined to him your expectations, O Empress. He is a wild donkey of a man, so I cannot guarantee a soft approach from him, but I think he knows he is corralled."

"All the same," Eudoxia grumbled, "I was over at Chalcedon in the church there. Rufinus the priest gave the most memorable sermon of Elisha pulling the axehead from the water. The allegory was so beautiful; the axehead is the promise of God, the water threatens to nullify its work, the wood Elisha threw in the water is God's grace to us, and the hand of the servant taking the axe head is our faith. Why can Chrysostom not paint his homilies so magically? Why must he preach so plainly?"

"I think he believes his straightforward approach handles the Scriptures more faithfully," Nicorious wondered

"What he calls faithful, I find hopelessly boring," Eudoxia yawned, fluffing her robe about her and adjusting the jeweled rings on her fingers. "Ah.! Here he comes now to grovel."

As Chrysostom ascended the pulpit, all eyes in the church turned to him, except the Empress who preferred to gossip with her entourage. Chrysostom stared up at the empress' box, disappointed at her behavior. Now it was his time to speak.

I will not deny you, Lord. He thought. I must obey God rather than men.

"I take as my text today," Chrysostom began, "the apostle Paul's words to the Corinthians in his first letter. I have spoken of how the apostle begs the church that they be imitators of him as he imitates Christ. The Corinthian church treated the Lord's Supper, our meal of the Lord's grace as a market tavern! Paul himself complains that 'one goes hungry, another gets drunk'. We too have allowed the Lord's meal to be an embarrassment through our entire city!

"What senselessness, what madness is this! We have so many poor standing within these walls today, and outside, and we have many who are wealthy who are unwilling to relieve even one among the poor. Are you who are noble and rich happy that you can relieve yourselves in silver pots at home, when those in threadbare rags who stand among you receive not even a crust of bread?"

The applause broke out, sections of the congregation stamping their feet and roaring with delight. Eudoxia glared at Chrysostom from her perch as he went on.

"The disdain with which you hold the poor of this city extends even to those who have come seeking a better life. You who call yourselves Christians, who revel in the blessings of wealth given you for a season, why do you ignore the Goths who live in filth and squalor within these streets? Does it delight you to see them on the brink of hell? Yes, they hold views of our Lord Jesus which require correction, but will you not join me in ministering to their needs of food, drink, and shelter, so that they might see the spirit of Christ and embrace Him truly? You shun them for their beliefs and will not allow them to belong amongst you? I say that belonging may precede believing. Extend them grace so they might find the Lord of grace! Yes, they are lost, and so were some of you! So are some of you!"

He drew himself up and stared into the smoldering eyes of Eudoxia. "The Word of God shows we must bow the knee to Christ above all, eliminating the idols of rich trappings and all that would eclipse our Saviour's gaze, resting in the protection of the Holy Spirit when we obey God rather than men, as the prophet Elijah did when he denounced idolatry in Israel. I declare to you today," he rasped as he pointed to the royal box, "that as Elijah rebuked Queen Jezebel in his own day, I rebuke her equivalent today! Christ is the head of His Church, and no human power can nor will change that!"

The roar was so loud it outstripped any sound Chrysostom had ever heard before, and he made his way down toward the cheering throng to the altar where the bread and wine of the Eucharist awaited his hands to serve.

"Chrysostom!" Nicorious' voice wavered from the door of the bishop's chamber.

"Yes?" asked Chrysostom, turning around and finding himself face to face with Empress Eudoxia, who had barged into the room. Her nostrils flaring, she strode toward the bishop, stopping with her face inches from his own.

"That little trick might have made you popular with the people, John," she leered, "but you are in my hands now, and your fate rests with me."

Chrysostom closed his eyes, offering a silent prayer, and then opened them to face his queen. "Empress, you deceive yourself to think I am in your hands. I rest in the hands of the Triune God, and I welcome my fate from Him as long as I am His child."

JOHN CHRYSOSTOM served as bishop of Antioch from 386 to 397 before being named bishop of Constantinople the following year. His gifted, simple, yet eloquent preaching earned him the nickname Chrysostom, which means "Golden Mouth." A believer in preaching the Scriptures in their natural meaning rather than by allegory, John preached through many books of the Bible. His moral courage and directness exposed the corruption and affluence of the ruling class and the clergy in the area. Falling out of favor with Empress Eudoxia, he was banished from Constantinople in 403, but popular uprisings by the people forced her to recall him later that year. Still, the palace never embraced his zeal for reform, and he endured dismissal and exile more times until his death in 407, always faithful in the midst of unjust attacks.

FACT FILES

Leo I and Papal Supremacy

Throughout the early years of Christianity, the Church could read within the pages of Scripture and discover the expectations that God had for their church leaders. While there were such skills needed as being able to teach, many of the qualifications were godly characteristics and morals. Leaders were to serve their local congregations, whether they were bishops, elders, or deacons. Because churches were scattered throughout the Roman Empire and beyond, the structure of Christianity was de-centralized; that is, spiritual direction and authority was more local in the individual churches, although Christians knew of other churches and prayed for them. Some leaders were more well-known through their writings, such as the apostles, along with bishops like Clement of Rome, Ignatius, and Cyprian, but for the most part, the bishop-leaders of the churches enjoyed a fairly level playing field, each generally viewed as equal in command and authority as the other. The bishop of Jerusalem was seen as a colleague of the bishop of Antioch, and Constantinople, and Ephesus, and so forth. It was a manageable structure at the time that spread out authority and spiritual care fairly evenly.

This worked well during the years of Christian persecution and lack of liberty. What created pressure on this system, ironically, was when Christianity became a tolerated and even championed religion within the Roman Empire. Now people entered the Church in greater numbers, but conflicts erupted, like the Arian controversy that forced the Council of Nicea. Conflict can give rise to the desire for strong leadership and clear champions of authority. The Church was no different in voicing these matters. What remained to be seen was which leader or city would claim a role over all others to have primacy, or supremacy, over other bishops.

Into this opening stepped Leo, whom history calls Pope Leo I or Leo the Great. Leo served as the bishop of Rome from 440 to 461, attaining much praise for his leadership of the Church, for his memorable sermons, his concern for the poor, his defense of the city of Rome in war, and his concern that bishops be servants to their people. It was at this time that the bishop of Rome became known by a name that would continue throughout history to the present day, pope. The word "pope" comes from the Latin "papa" and Greek "pappas", for "father", and the bishop of Rome increasingly became viewed as the spiritual father of Christians in the Latin West. Leo was not the first bishop of Rome to use the title of Pope, but he was the one who developed its meaning and implications beyond what anyone had before, leaving a lasting legacy for future generations.

On 29 September 443, the third anniversary of when he began his reign as Pope, Leo gave a sermon in Rome in which he put forth the reasons why the Pope should have power and authority over all other bishops. This seems like a prideful stance, but Leo himself was not an arrogant man. He actually spoke openly of his sins and need for constant forgiveness, and he never claimed to be a better Christian than anyone else. What sets apart the position of the Pope, he claimed, is the place of Peter. He referred to Jesus' praise of Peter's confession of faith in Christ in Matthew 16, in which Jesus tells Peter that "you are Peter, and upon this rock I will build My church, and the gates of hell shall not prevail against it. I will give you the keys of the kingdom of heaven, and whatever you bind on earth, shall be bound in heaven; and whatever you loose on earth, shall be loosed in heaven." Leo went on to state that Peter, having come to Rome, became the foundation of the Church there, its patron. Peter was the rock on which the Church would be built. The bishops of Rome follow in succession from Peter's time as the first Pope, said Leo, and since they follow the one on whom Christ said He would build His Church, the bishops of Rome have "the chief honor of this service" and the Pope was "the primate of all bishops."

While Leo was confident in what he said, not everyone fell in line with his statements. Many other bishops showed resistance to this idea and were content to have authority over their own patch but not give supreme honor to Rome. Six hundred years later, this would result in a vicious clash between Rome and Constantinople that led to a savage break between the Western and Eastern Christian churches (more of that to come in a later book!).

As history unfolded, Leo's ideas took many twists and turns. Sometimes Leo used the force of his personality to shape decisions. When confusion about Jesus' divinity and humanity erupted, Leo pressed upon the Empress Pulcheria to call a council at Chalcedon to settle the matter, exerting his sense of primacy over other bishops. Years later, Pope Gelasius I would expand this notion of papal supremacy to say that the Church has greater authority than human government in the lives of people. As the Western Church moved through the Middle Ages, there were significant clashes between some popes on one hand and kings on the other in a struggle over who had greater authority. There were a number of popes who were strong leaders who exercised their authority with confidence (and perhaps too much strength); others were weak popes who were overwhelmed by their calling.

Today, the issue of papal supremacy is one of the dividing points between the Roman Catholic Church the Eastern Orthodox Churches and Protestants. The Orthodox Churches reject one bishop over all the faithful and view their archbishops (or patriarchs) has having equal and shared authority. While Catholics maintain that the pope's authority comes from Peter as the rock on which the Church was built, many Protestants firmly teach the "rock" of which Jesus spoke in Matthew 16 was not Peter himself but his expression of faith in Christ. Salvation in Jesus, therefore, is the foundation of the Church, not one individual.

When Leo uttered the doctrine of papal supremacy in 443, he likely had no idea what his vision would unleash in future years. In fairness to Leo, no one has that kind of foresight. Would he have been more cautious if he could consider the implications of his teaching? Did his vision for Church leadership move beyond the structure of the New Testament and early church? We could answer "perhaps" to both of those questions. It is true that Leo's view created challenges as well as opportunities for the Church into the future, even as his deep love for Christ's people motivated him to be the most faithful shepherd for the Church as he could possibly be.

JEROME

Autumn of 410, Bethlehem

The marketplace of Bethlehem came alive with the harvest every year. The plainly-dressed, white-bearded fellow tottered through the maze of booths on this Thursday afternoon, clutching a cloth bag in his right hand. Beside him walked a lady, some twenty years his junior. In spite of her relative youth and strength, she found it difficult to keep up with him through the market and, losing sight of him for a brief moment, called out, "Father Jerome! Father Jerome!"

The monk turned toward the sound of desperation and raised his hand above the swirling, chattering crowd, waving in his direction. A few moments later, his female friend arrived at his side, harried and worn out in the warmth of the day. "I will be glad when the sun goes down and gives way to cooler temperatures, Jerome, but no matter how much light it gives, I can't use it to track your movements. Are you trying to escape from me?"

"I am sorry, dear Sister Eustochium," Jerome offered in return, a slight smile creasing his otherwise solemn face. "I was distracted by something."

"One of the booths?" Eustochium asked.

Jerome waved off the suggestion even as he pointed to a table heaped with gourds and roots. "Over here. Let's find something for our supper tonight. No, it wasn't anything here in the market. It was the strangest feeling. I received a sense of foreboding, as if something deeply wrong and tragic had happened."

"Here in Bethlehem?" replied Eustochium as she took the bag from the absent-minded Jerome and pressed several coins in the hands of the merchant, who filled the sack with plenty of vegetables.

"That is the oddest thing, my child," Jerome muttered as they turned back the way they came, heading down the main street of the city. "It has nothing to do with here. Nothing that will threaten our communities, at least not now. But there was a clutch of darkness that gripped my heart. I normally get those when deeply aware of the presence of horrible sin in my soul, but I have spent the morning in confession before my Saviour. It might not make sense, but I am deeply afraid that we will be receiving some terrible, terrible news."

Eustochium shook her head as she whipped the sack around her shoulder to carry the vegetables home. "I have sat under your teaching for many years now, dear Father Jerome, and I have always had an abiding conviction from the Holy Spirit that you were always led in the truth for our sakes." She paused.

"And now?" Jerome asked as his walk slowed to a shuffle when the monasteries appeared before them.

"I pray this time," she replied, "that you are completely wrong."

The dinner that night was a simple affair. Many of the younger monks took care to cook the sliced roots and gourds over the flame in a thin coating of oil. Jerome was competent if somewhat fussy about the process, but his oversight was hardly needed and he was able to lend a hand to the women as they baked the barley bread.

"You are quite serious about the oil, blessed father!" called one of the monastery cooks by the oven.

"I have to be, Gallus," Jerome nodded. "I had read and written about another holy man, Hilarion, who sought to maintain his health with vegetables only, barely cooked in plain water. He believed the Lord would honor his attempts at frugality in his diet."

"So why do we conduct our meals this way?" Gallus asked. "We've been cooking with oil since I arrived here five years ago."

"And well before," Jerome smiled, patting Gallus on the arm, and peering into the oven to ensure things were progressing nicely. "Hilarion discovered that his sight was failing, and his skin became rather tough and rigid. It seemed clear that this approach to dining was not a wise one, and thus he began cooking his food in oil. His sight returned to its normal vigor and his skin healed properly. I thank the Lord every day that I discovered Hilarion's plight and that he prevented me from journeying down that foolish road. Our King of Heaven, Gallus, rules over all things, including our needs for daily bread."

Just then a scream pierced the streets of Bethlehem outside, followed by others. The clamor of feet pounding the roads could be heard at the monastery, and several of the monks looked outside. "See all the people rushing to the center of town!" exclaimed another monk.

Jerome rushed to the window and, looking downward, saw Eustochium run from the lower chamber of her monastery. "Stay here," he said to the other monks, "and take your food. I will return to you."

But he had just turned back to look outside the window when he saw a frail, weeping man limping toward their building, leaning heavily on Eustochium's arm. Jerome peered closely through the twilight and saw who it was. And the clutch to his heart returned.

"Pacificus!" Jerome gasped as his friend entered the doorway and collapsed to the floor. "Whatever has brought you here? Eustochium," he turned to her, "go and fetch water and a little bread so he can regain his strength."

"There is no strength left to regain!" gasped Pacificus, dropping his staff to the ground. "Jerome! Jerome, my friend! There is nothing to regain. I have traveled for forty days to tell you that, for I barely escaped with my life!"

"But you were in Rome the last I knew of your whereabouts, Pacificus!" Jerome stammered. "How could you have escaped? Pagans did not attack you, did they?"

"Attack me? If only they had merely done that!" Pacificus sobbed. "If only I had died while the jewel of the world could still shine forth! She has fallen, Jerome! Sacked and looted! Rome has fallen to the barbarians."

Jerome collapsed face first to the ground. His arms quivered as he tried to raise his body up again. Rome, he thought, the place where the Pope dwells. Where the Church shines forth. Where the knowledge of the ages blazed through the Empire!

He staggered to his feet and saw the sun dip from view on the western horizon, plunging the sky into the same kind of darkness he felt in his soul.

"Rome," he whispered as he felt Eustochium's hand on his shoulder, "the city that conquered the world, has itself been conquered." And he wept.

"In the end," Pacificus sniffed between bites of bread and sips of water, "perhaps holding out for nearly two years was the best we could do. Alaric and his Visigoth hordes were powerful, skilled, and organized. Priests proclaimed we would triumph in the end, that the Lord Jesus would never allow a city to fall to Arian heretics. But it was all for nothing. We have not walked in a manner worthy of the Lord Jesus. Even the pope himself was willing to allow people to offer pagan rituals to the old gods to keep Alaric at bay, as long as they acted privately."

"Some of those priests are likely the worldly scamps that I railed against upon leaving the city," Jerome mused sadly. "The pope, however, knows better than to compromise the Gospel in such manner. And to say that Christ would not leave Rome defenseless is all too near the overconfidence of the Hebrews who took the ark of the covenant into battle against the Philistines. They used it as a charm for fortune...no wonder Almighty God allowed their defeat. And He has willingly allowed this one. But how did Alaric's army break through?"

"Emperor Honorius reneged on the tribute paid to Alaric, and Sarus the Goth allied himself with Honorius and attacked Alaric's force on open ground. Alaric was so furious by the deception that he marched on Rome and laid a siege that broke us completely. In the end, they came through the Salarian Gate in full force."

"From the northeast," Jerome wept softly. "I thought that gate to be impenetrable."

"I heard from a friend that desperate folk starved for food opened it. I hid near St. Peter's Church until it was clear the marauders would stop at nothing in their pillaging. They destroyed the mausoleums of the emperors, took gold and silver from every building they could, overpowered and killed citizens, and took numerous slaves. I managed to outrun them to the south gate and galloped away to Ostia. By ship and land, I have come away to bear the news to you. It is over. O Jerome, all hope is over!"

And for the first time that day, a ray of light flooded Jerome's heart. He reached down and lifted his friend to his feet.

"No, Pacificus," he replied. "Rome may be conquered, but our hope is not snuffed out. Come with me, and I will show you."

Pacificus' jaw dropped when he saw the pages, turned one after the other, gleaming by the light of the lamp. To think that his friend had devoted so much time to this, and now this gift for the entire Church, sat here in this room.

"The entire Bible," Pacificus sighed, hardly believing what he beheld. "You have done it, Jerome! Such an achievement, and it has taken you so long to complete it! How did you manage?"

"Discipline and the Lord's favor," Jerome admitted, the weariness of the day covering him like a heavy blanket. "You of course recall when Pope Damasus commissioned me to undertake it."

"That was twenty-eight years ago!" Pacificus exclaimed. "After we had gone back to Rome from Antioch. And then you left the city not long after that!"

"Eventually to end up here by way of the desert," Jerome grimaced, "but always I was thinking about the Scriptures. The Word of God in the original translations of man. For years I wondered why I loved Greek and Hebrew, especially Hebrew, with such a passion. And the Holy Spirit made that increasingly clear once I sat down to translate."

"It is all here!" Pacificus marveled as he turned page after page. "The Books of the Law, Joshua, Samuel and Kings, the Psalms, the many prophets! And all in the Latin tongue."

"We require a standard by which the priests can read and understand the Scriptures, Pacificus," Jerome replied. "Not all understand Hebrew. Not all can read Greek. But Latin should be another matter. I pray this fills a great need for the Church. For the past five years since its completion, I have heard from many who believe it is doing just that."

Pacificus closed the volume and sat across from his friend. "Do you think the priests will readily take up your treasure, Jerome? It is the crying need of the hour, but you have not been back to Rome for many years, and you left with many relations somewhat frayed."

"For which I pray forgiveness for my tone, if not my message," Jerome frowned. "I cannot abide the vices in which many Roman priests willingly indulged themselves. Wine, women, and wild debauchery. I will never apologize for raising the alarm, even if leaders were slow to respond to my cautions. But I speak bluntly with little love. One thing that I have since learned is that a sharp bite can be encased in soft silk. I can still hate sin but show compassion. It is a lesson I am still learning."

"Regarding sin?"

"Regarding my heart, Pacificus. I always believed that it was important to live a disciplined life, a gift we may offer to our risen Lord. And to achieve that, I went out into the desert. Tired of the revelry of Rome, of the suggestive women, I believed that if I withdrew from the world, I would become pure like Christ. And nothing of the sort happened."

"It had no effect?"

"I could run from Rome. I could flee sinful trappings and carnal desire, Pacificus. But I could not outrun the lusts and vices of my own heart. The words of Jeremiah haunted me: 'The heart is deceitful above all things.' And that is what drove me to found this community here in Bethlehem, to draw strength from fellow believers who confess their sin to one another."

Pacificus looked back to the translated copy of the Scriptures on the table. "As difficult as that is to hear, Jerome, I am thankful that you have placed the Word of God within the reach of those who lead His people. Rome has fallen to heretics and barbarians but I thank God has given us this gift that will combat the darkness."

Jerome looked outside into the darkness of Bethlehem. "I often take solace in the story of creation. It says that each day there was evening and there was morning. Darkness holds for a time, but is always followed by light. I have been a brutish man in the days I have walked this earth, speaking harshly when I should temper my speech and forgetting my heart is a spring of all sorts of evil. But above all, I have become more and more thankful that God is willing to work through a wretched sinner such as myself. And if He can bring light out of my own darkness, I believe He will do so throughout His world, however long it might stand."

JEROME's most significant achievement is the translation of the Bible into Latin, a volume called the Vulgate because it was in the common language of the day. He also was a historian and Biblical scholar who compiled many commentaries on individual books of Scripture. A dedicated monk and hermit, Jerome gathered a community of like-minded followers, both men and women, in Bethlehem and discipled them, encouraging them in Scripture and a strict godly life. Jerome lived ten years after Alaric's conquest of Rome and, soon after the death of Eustochium, he entered his heavenly reward at the end of September 420.

AUGUSTINE

May 418, Carthage, North Africa

The double rainbow soared overhead, as if placing itself as a colored arch over the cathedral just north of Byrsa Hill. More than a dozen men trudged over the paths, slick with the remnants of the unusual rainstorm that had dropped the outdoor temperature some fifteen degrees. Strong, swirling winds were pushing out toward the Mediterranean Sea, but head down and lost in his thoughts, Augustine pulled his purple robe around him to ward off the chills invading his sixty-three-year-old body. All he could think of now was the looming battle that was coming in the church, and he had to be ready.

"Augustine!" he heard someone call from the direction of the church. Looking up, he saw his friend and fellow bishop Possidius[1] scurrying over the soaked cobbles while remarkably keeping his balance. Raising a finger and pointing to the far side of the church, Augustine urged his friend to the north side of the cathedral for whatever needed to be said. Possidius came to his side and looked back at the other bishops while continuing to walk with his colleague.

"This has been a greater challenge than I believed necessary, my good Augustine," Possidius grunted as he wiped his forehead.

"Is the challenge you speak of the council before us?" Augustine remarked. "Or is it this unseasonably cool blast and rainfall?"

1. Friend of Augustine's and bishop of Calama in the Roman province of Numidia (modern-day Algeria).

"Different from what you would expect at Hippo and what I would have in Calama," Possidius agreed. "But that is not why I have come to you just now."

"We have come to you just now," came the voice of another who circled around the pillar on the northwest corner of the church and approached the men.

"Alypius," Augustine nodded toward him to acknowledge the bishop's presence. "Well, here we have the shepherds of the faithful in Hippo, Calama, and Tagaste. What is the purpose of this secret gathering?"

"It has to do with bringing this council to a definitive close," Alypius sighed, his neatly-trimmed gray beard contrasting with the longer, wilder versions that Augustine and Possidius both possessed. "We have listened to one another, and even the pope has already condemned our opponents."

"Alypius speaks the truth," said Possidius. "Pope Zosimus sent his official letter that finally declared Pelagius' views as heresy. Now we are having this council, and Pelagius' disciples will have a chance to speak yet again."

"Yes" Augustine agreed, "but as long as people promote false teaching, we must refute them."

"All this we have been doing," Alypius wearily replied. "But Julian Caelo continues to fight for his master, Pelagius. And we are growing tired. We need you to bring this to a definite conclusion."

"Because you are tired?" Augustine asked.

"Because you are the premier theologian, the greatest thinker from these shores and throughout the Christian world, Augustine!" exclaimed Possidius. "And if anyone can ward off the words of Julian Caelo and expose their falsehood, you can!"

Augustine stood quietly for several moments, looking from Possidius to Alypius, and then finally he replied.

"Yes, it is a time to speak, my friends," he began. "But we have been over the Scriptures with a sure tongue and skilled reason. Julian Caelo and his few supporters also have raised Scripture and will continue to do so. He believes he can use God's Word to prove his master's teaching. We must demonstrate that, above all, the Word of God is living and active."

"What do you mean, Augustine?" Possidius asked. "What are you proposing?"

Augustine began walking toward the cathedral's doors, signaling his fellow bishops to come with him, speaking low with every stride. "I mean that we consider two things. First, the most powerful words in our world are, 'Thus says the Lord'. What our Lord speaks in His Word is no doubt true. But we must go to where Pelagius' followers will not go, that God's Word transforms, for the most penetrating words of our age are 'This is what the Lord has done for me!' And that is what I intend to do."

"What is that, Augustine?" Alypius inquired as they entered the cathedral.

"I will tell them my own story," Augustine replied, "of how Jesus Christ rescued me, not because I found Him, but because there was no other way."

The cathedral was drafty inside. Augustine wrapped his robe even more tightly around him as he sat quietly in the nave, listening intently as Julian Caelo completed his winding case in defense of Pelagius' teaching. The wind outside picked up, and Augustine sniffed at the air, wondering if the rain might chance a return.

"Esteemed brothers in Christ," Caelo proclaimed with a flourish, "we are not asking you to abstain from your teaching, only that you affirm ours as a legitimate affirmation of God's nature and ours. God is our Father, not a cruel judge, and so how can we not think of Him as drawing, wooing us to Him. He gives certain and clear evidence of Himself, to be sure, as Augustine has demonstrated from Paul's words to the Christians in Rome. But whereas Augustine and many of you declare that God must place us in His grasp for us to enter His kingdom, we proclaim that God is so loving that He willingly surrenders absolute control and desires us to come to Him, whether we require grace or, in some cases, not. In the end, we step to the Lord Jesus, rather than He to us. It is this way from the beginning of life, when we are born with no smudge or spot to our name, free to choose God or reject Him. To say sin originates with Adam and is passed on to us is to fly in the face of God's nature. For how else could God be a God of love if He did not wish that our love for Him be unforced, without compulsion, without imposition? Could He truly be God otherwise?"

The nods and smattering of applause came from the few among them in support of Caelo, but Augustine wasted no time springing to his feet.

"My Reverend Father Aurelius," he began, "may I request permission to speak?"

"Go ahead, my son," the bishop of Carthage waved him forward. Augustine turned to the dozens in the nave and set his eyes upon the gathering of bishops. This is it, he thought. I must be both gracious and firm. The very Gospel is at stake.

"I could come before you today, my brothers in the faith, and match Caelo phrase for phrase, line for line, from prophecy, narrative, psalm, or epistle. Today, however, I will not do so, for two reasons. One, I have done so many times over the past several days. But there is a second reason, namely, that I know of the surpassing, absolutely necessary grace of Christ Himself, that I receive his free and undeserved love and favor that saves me from sin! I know it because I have lived it. For me, there was no other way to come into His embrace, unless He drew me wholly Himself."

Augustine began to pace the floor. Aurelius smiled, knowing his friend always did this when he got excited. Augustine continued, "All these things I have written of in my Confessions. I admit that the great Ambrose, through persuasion and clear teaching from Scripture, brought me to the face of God. But the bishop had done so in spite of my resistance. There was no desire I would not indulge, there was no woman I would not seek, and there was no passion I would refuse. In spite of my desire for human wisdom, I constantly prayed to God, 'Grant me chastity and discipline, but not for the moment.' Yes, a prayer, to be sure, but there was no sincerity whatsoever."

"Perhaps you should have looked elsewhere, good Augustine," Caelo blurted out with a toothy grin. "The evil around us afflicts us, not any sin dwelling in us! Maybe you just need to realize the truth that you are not an evil man, but rather are a good man who faces the threats of evil."

"Sadly, your words show how little you know me, Caelo," Augustine retorted, bringing murmurs from the other bishops. "At no point did the evil around me drag me toward the pit of rebellion. I was the pit of rebellion! My dear mother Monica prayed earnestly for me and still I stumbled toward sin more and more. Don't the Scriptures say, 'As a dog returns to its vomit, so a fool returns to his folly'? I was a foolish dog from when I was born, undeniable evidence that David spoke the words of the Holy Spirit when he wrote, 'I was sinful from birth, sinful from the moment my mother conceived me.'"

The murmurs grew louder. Augustine went on. "If you claim that we can find our way to God without divine grace, then why indeed does grace leap off every page of Scripture? If we can morally conform ourselves to the will of God, then isn't the cross of our Lord Jesus a cruel and savage and meaningless punishment?"

"Think of what you are saying, Augustine!" Caelo exclaimed. "How can we be held responsible for sin we haven't committed but are stained with? Why would God place such a burden upon us? Why would he give us more than we could bear?"

"I think what you find, Caelo," Augustine responded, "is that is precisely what God allows. The life I live covered by the blood of Christ is one of immeasurable hardship, in which I find myself unable to do so much. But therein we find the grace of the Lord falling upon us like gentle rain! He never grants us challenges greater than His power! To overcome our sin and seek His face is beyond our desire or ability! Sin is not merely something you can choose to do or not do; it is a power which holds you in its grip! You can bemoan what you perceive to be injustice, Caelo. I only know this to be true, for I was in the clutches of sin and in bondage to the kingdom of Satan, and only Christ in His grace could set me free!"

The pacing continued, the murmurs grew louder, and Augustine raised his hands. "Thirty-two years ago, in Milan, I experienced that of which I speak. I wandered absent-mindedly through a garden, my heart running from the call of Christ even as I yearned for peace. A large hedge stood behind me when I heard, as if it was a chant in a child's voice. 'Take up and read,' he said, 'take up and read.'

The nearest volume I could find was the writings of the apostle Paul to the Romans. At random I opened to those convicting and heart-searing words, 'Let us walk properly as in the daytime, not in orgies and drunkenness, not in sexual immorality and sensuality, not in quarreling and jealousy. But put on the Lord Jesus Christ, and make no provision for the flesh, to gratify its desires.'

I tell you this, that only Jesus could dress me in his righteousness. Only He could wash me by His blessed blood. Only He could draw me to His blessed, life-giving Word. If I am to be saved, I am not only saved to a glorious hope, but I am also saved from a devastating ruin."

"This is outrageous," Caelo rose from his seat, the veins in his temples slightly bulging. "You speak of grace with lofty joy," he barked, "yet if God truly draws us to Him, and this is no manner of our doing, then what possible motivation do we have for holiness?"

"My master Pelagius was grieved by the loose living and laxity he saw around him in Rome," declared Caelo, "even from so-called Christians! If you hold to your teaching, Augustine, that divine grace is our only hope, that we are saved from ruin by God and contribute nothing, why should we not grow fat and lazy and ignore the law of God? Can you plainly show me?"

And here Augustine looked quite pained. He sat down and waved Caelo to join him in being seated. "My good Caelo, my issue is with the words and teaching of Pelagius. I feel great pain for him. I love the man himself, but I am concerned with the falsehood he teaches. There are few who live as godly a life as Pelagius does. But you have asked a question, and this answer I give you in closing.

"Imagine a barbarian army attacked your beloved city, and you were trapped by an advancing column of armed men, Goths, Vandals, whatever. Death is certain but a lone guard of your hometown leapt into the fray, countering the barbarian charge, and giving you a chance to escape to safety. As you look back and see the guard cut down by the enemy, a brave soul who perished unselfishly. You did not ask for that. You did not deserve that. But he fought that you may escape. He died that you might live. Throughout the remainder of your days, would you dare to throw away and scoff at your freedom won by the price of his blood? Or would you, set free by his death, not live in such a way that it demonstrated thanksgiving for his sacrifice, which you did not earn?"

Augustine looked around at the bishops, all of whom had fallen silent under the spell of his words. "True grace will never bear its own cheapening, or it cannot be grace at all. I am not a sinner because I sin; I sin because I am a hopeless sinner. But Christ fell to raise me up, and He lives so I may live for Him. And if you intend to say that we can find Him when we are spiritually blind, Caelo, then the Church of Christ should be the most pitied band of people on earth."

He turned to Aurelius, extending his palm to his fellow bishop. "And this is where I take my determined place, as a rebel whom God has sought and chosen. Now we all must decide whose view of God will win the day."

At the Council of Carthage in 418, the teaching of **AUGUSTINE** on the original sin of humans, together with the absolute necessity that God's grace draws us to salvation, won the day. The greatest theologian of the late ancient Church, Augustine was converted to the Christian faith out of a wild season of sin and rebellion, was mentored by Ambrose of Milan, and eventually became the bishop of Hippo Regius (in modern-day Algeria) on the North African coast. He wrote his spiritual autobiography, *Confessions*, which has become a classic, as well as *The City of God* to demonstrate how Christians live under both human and divine government in this world. Augustine's influence over the late ancient and medieval Church was so great that the history of Western Christianity in the Middle Ages can rightly be seen as the story of how the world interpreted his teaching. In later years, Augustine's teaching on God's undeserved, essential, and effective grace spearheaded the Protestant Reformation under Martin Luther and John Calvin.

FACT FILES

Ancient Church Councils

In the early seventeenth century, an English bishop named Lancelot Andrewes looked back upon the ancient church to emphasize what held Christians together in their common beliefs. Andrewes famously declared that "one canon, two testaments, three creeds, four councils, and five centuries determine the boundary of our faith."

What did he mean by that, you might ask? Well, the one canon would be the Bible, in which is contained the two testaments of Old and New. Andrewes also affirmed the three creeds known as the Apostles', Nicene, and Athanasian Creeds, and he also believed that whatever matters were vital for all Christians to believe, they occurred in the first five centuries after Christ's birth.

That leaves one number that you might have noticed I skipped over: What are the four councils? Very briefly, they are the Councils of Nicea, Constantinople, Ephesus, and Chalcedon.

In truth, there have been many church councils throughout history. The earliest one we have recorded in the Bible was the Council at Jerusalem in Acts 15, where Christian leaders dealt with how exactly non-Jewish Christians would be welcomed and strengthened in the Church. A more modern church council would be the Second Vatican Council of the Catholic Church from 1962-1965. Church councils occur as formal assemblies of bishops and church representatives, in which they seek to define biblical teaching or to deal with some serious conflict about doctrine or morals. Andrewes looked back on four specific ancient church councils as critically important because they were the first ecumenical councils. This means these meetings are attended by representatives throughout the Christian world and have implications for the entire Church. So, if these councils are important, what were their results?

We have already taken a peek at the events of the Council of Nicea in the chapter on Athanasius. The emperor Constantine had granted freedom of worship to Christians throughout the Roman Empire. This freedom brought on more open discussion and debate of church teaching on different issues. In Alexandria, Egypt, vicious disputes broke out over who Jesus was. Arius, a pastor, taught that Jesus was not the eternal Son of God and was the first created being. If Jesus was the Son of God, He could not be the equal of God the Father. Athanasius, the bishop's assistant who would be the future bishop of Alexandria, saw the devastating consequences of this teaching. If Jesus was created and wasn't God, we couldn't worship Him, nor could we depend upon His death to secure our salvation from sin! And why did Jesus receive prayer and worship in the New Testament? Why did biblical writers declare Jesus' divine nature if He wasn't eternally God? The arguments were so strong they threatened to rip the Empire apart, so Constantine, who desired order, called for a council at Nicea in 325 to settle the matter. As Athanasius' powerful arguments went forth at Nicea, the tide turned in favor of affirming Jesus as the eternal Son of God. The bishops drafted (and most of them signed) what became known as the Nicene Creed, which states clearly that Jesus is "the only-begotten Son of God, eternally begotten of the Father...true God from true God, begotten, not made, of one substance with the Father."

In spite of the apparent victory of Athanasius and his supporters at Nicea, the Arian faction managed to find sympathetic emperors and rulers throughout the Roman Empire over the next half-century, securing places of power and influence in many urban centers. Confusion reigned once again. In defense of Jesus' eternal divine nature arose three great theologians: Basil of Caesarea, Gregory of Nyssa, and Gregory of Nazianzus. Together known as the Great Cappadocians, they labored on behalf of what Athanasius fought for at Nicea. In time, Gregory of Nazianzus was named bishop of Constantinople, and in 381 he was asked by Emperor Theodosius I to preside over the Council of Constantinople. Gregory disliked the conflict that flooded the meeting; he complained that the assembled bishops behaved like a swarm of hornets. But Theodosius maintained that they must reach consensus, and the council's labors proved fruitful in the end. At last, the doctrine of Jesus' eternal divine nature triumphed, and the assembly affirmed an expanded, finalized edition of the original Nicene Creed. Also, the bishops discussed the person and work of the Holy Spirit. Pointing out that God sends the Spirit into the world to continue Jesus' work (John 14:26), the Holy Spirit presents our prayers to the Father (Romans 8:27), and that when people lie to the Holy Spirit, they are lying to God, the bishops affirmed the divine nature of the Holy Spirit, as well. This was an important moment in the Church, for now Christians confirmed that God exists as a Trinity: Father, Son, and Holy Spirit.

Questions about Jesus did not cease, however. The speculation turned from "Is Jesus eternally God?" to "If Jesus is God and human, then how do these natures fit together?" Bishops and pastors desperately tried to come up with formulas that would capture Jesus' identity with accuracy, but it led them into some dangerous areas. Apollinaris was a bishop in Laodecia who thought the way to explain Jesus' identity was to divide Him up into parts. He declared that a perfect divine being and perfect human being cannot exist in one person, so there must be a division within Jesus. He claimed Jesus had a human body, a human soul, but a divine mind. Other leaders were quick to point out the problems with this view. If Jesus was not fully divine, how could He remain sinless on our behalf as He lived? And if Jesus was not fully human, how could He properly represent us on the Cross in His death? Apollinaris' views were condemned at Constantinople, but after several years the teachings of Nestorius arose. Nestorius had recently been named the bishop of Constantinople, but he offered some confusing ideas about Jesus. He claimed that Jesus had a human person in his body, along with a divine person. This raised several questions? Is Jesus perfectly human? Is He perfectly God? Wasn't Jesus God who came to earth and was incarnate (became flesh) by being born to Mary? The questions were severe enough for Emperor Theodosius II to call for the Council of Ephesus in 431. There, Nestorius labored to explain his views, which did not properly show how Jesus was truly God and truly human. Cyril, the bishop of Alexandria, condemned Nestorius' views and the defeated bishop was stripped of his title and role.

Ephesus did not give final clarity to the question of Jesus, for in the fifth century another thinker arose, a pastor from Constantinople named Eutyches. Seeking to preserve Jesus' lordship and unique place in Christianity, Eutyches declared that when Jesus was born of the Virgin Mary, His divine and human natures at some point ceased to be separate and instead fused into a new, single, combined nature in one body. This view was given several names such as monophysitism (one body) or monothelitism (one will). Eutyches also said that Jesus was "of one substance with the Father, but not of one substance with us." The same questions that had been leveled at Apollinaris seventy years before came back full force. Pope Leo I (mentioned earlier in this book) wanted the question dealt with once and for all, and in 451 the Empress Pulcheria made it known she wanted as many bishops as possible to meet in what would be known as the Council of Chalcedon (Nicea, Constantinople, and Chalcedon are all within a short distance from each other). There, Eutyches' views were condemned while the bishops made a monumental decision. They would draft another document: a creed used to define the doctrine of Jesus' dual natures. Instead of specifying all the details which people must believe, the bishops rather "defined" the boundaries beyond which a Christian should not go in believing who Jesus is. The Definition of Chalcedon affirmed everything that the Nicene Creed had previously stated, plus Chalcedon described Jesus Christ as two natures unified in one person, genuinely human and completely divine, the perfect God-man. The bishops agreed that Jesus Christ was completely like God and completely like us, except for our sin. Some churches in the Eastern portion of the Empire continued to follow the doctrines that Ephesus and Chalcedon had condemned. The followers of Eutyches were the Monophysites, concentrated in Egypt and Syria, whereas the followers of Nestorious were concentrated in Persia. Still, regarding the question of "Who is Jesus Christ?", most of the Christian church had settled the matter. As Lancelot Andrewes would wistfully say centuries later, we had confirmed the boundaries of our faith.

PATRICK

432, Irish coast near Wicklow

Holding his cowl tightly around his body to rebuff the force of the gale, Drustan fought to get the fire going on the beach. The damp wood was taking forever to light, and the sticks were proving useless for the proper friction needed to spark a flame. If we don't eat soon, I will die of hunger, Drustan thought, and then Patrick will have to continue on alone.

"Drustan!" Patrick called as he hobbled toward the wood pile. The priest was clutching something under his heavy robe, but Drustan could not make it out until Patrick approached and pressed some dry sticks into his hands.

"English fir branches," Patrick smiled, his voice ringing with joy. "I had them hidden under the blanket in the boat. I know you have to be frustrated it comes to this, but I was waiting to see if anything here would start the fire."

"These will do, sire," Drustan admitted, "but it would also help if you'd brought the..."

Patrick reached under his cloak once more and pulled out a fabric-wrapped bundle. "Fish?"

Drustan smiled at Patrick's flair for the dramatic. The wind pounded the beach as the fog rolled over them. "Let me see if I can get this fire going and block the wind at the same time. Beastly weather to have breakfast in, if you ask me."

Patrick raised his eyes, then gently admonished his young traveler. "Better than having rain, as well."

In spite of Drustan's worry, the fir branches stoked the flame, and within the hour they had a delicious breakfast of fish and apples that they had roasted on the ends of wooden sticks. Patrick sat contentedly in the sand as Drustan continued to warm himself by the fire before the young man broke the companionable silence.

"I am still baffled at your desire to return here, Brother Patrick," he began. "First of all, we didn't get the best reception further south when we landed. Secondly, the weather is hardly a welcoming feature."

"Yes," Patrick replied thoughtfully, the wind starting to abate. "The townspeople might have been surprised at the sight of a boat and two strange travelers at twilight. No doubt, when more of our party arrives, also without weapons, they will realize this is no invasion of their kingdom. But the chieftains can be rather territorial, Drustan. I will not expect open arms. Now, as far as the weather goes, it is a particularly harsh morning, but I would wager in two hours' time both clouds and wind will disperse. And the views on a clear day are quite stunning. I recall how one can look across the sea and view Gwynedd[1] and the mountains. I think you may be romanticizing the weather back home, which is hardly ideal."

Drustan looked pensive. "Brother Patrick, you urged me to come with you ahead of the other monks, but you haven't fully told me why. Why here? Why Ireland? I know you spent some time here, but why would we leave Britain to come to this patch of ground when there are Druids ready to sacrifice us on sight?"

"Oh, we would have to go further into the rolling hills to encounter Druids, although wouldn't you agree they need to hear of the risen Christ just as anyone does?"

"I do not doubt your sincerity, Brother Patrick. I am confused about why we begin here."

---

1. An ancient name for Wales.

It was Patrick's turn to look pensive. "Because this is where my story began years ago. You know that I was a slave, but I did not serve back in Luguvalium[2], nor in Cornwall[3], nor Ulster[4]. No, I was taken a year before your birth, by pirates who came from these shores, and I was brought here against my will."

"All the way here!" Drustan exclaimed. "Did your family wonder about you?"

"I am certain of it," Patrick replied, "but how would they have discovered where I was? I was brought here and served a Druid chieftain named Oengus for six years. He was not brutal to me; there were no beatings, but he belittled me so. Eventually, he sent me out to the field to tend his sheep, and I spent many hours alone, herding them and chasing the recalcitrant ones to bring them back to safety."

"It was rather hard fortune for you to be stuck with that lot," Drustan uttered.

"As the world thinks, that might be true," Patrick spoke, looking out to the sea, "but I do believe that like Moses in the wilderness, God had a purpose to shackle me to the pasture. During the many hours I spent alone, the Lord showed his mercies to me. Although my father ministered as a curate and my grandfather served Christ as a priest, I was a wayward, wandering youth with little time or desire to seek the way of the Cross. Now I was here in Ireland, enslaved to a man who despised the Lord Jesus, and I sat in the fields day after day. I came to see that Christ was the only hope I had! The Lord had mercy upon me for my youthful ignorance, and all I could do while alone was pray. I would pray, 'Christ, if you see me, draw me to you. Though my arms be weak, may your arms encircle me.' And I believed, Drustan! I believed."

2. A Roman town in northern Britain.

3. A historic county in South West England.

4. One of four traditional Irish provinces in the North of Ireland.

"Then how did you end up back home?"

"Ah, that! A fortuitous event, that was. One night as I slept in the middle of a time of fasting from food, I heard a voice, clear as a bell and soft as a snowfall, utter the words 'You do well to fast. Soon you will depart for your home country.' I started awake and wondered if I had dreamed the whole thing. I decided to make another attempt at sleep again when a voice prophesied in the darkness, 'Behold! Your ship is ready!'"

"A ship?"

"Yes, Drustan, a ship. And so I left, traveling many days and over many miles until I found the ships, for it was nowhere about this region. Six years I had served my master and that night I removed myself and left, returning home to serve Christ, to teach His people, and to nurture their faith."

Drustan looked upward, noting the clouds had parted and a sliver of the sun poked through the clouds. "Yes, you've been doing that with exceeding grace and skill, Brother Patrick. So why are we here in Ireland, with that passion in your heart to return?"

"Yes, that was another vision."

"Another..."

"Another vision, my friend. One night a year ago, I stood outside. I saw a man coming toward me from the west, from Ireland. Don't ask me how I knew, but he wore the sash of an Irish noble and bore a cross on his forehead, and he carried many letters. He approached me and placed one in my hands, saying, 'On behalf of the lost and hungry, I, Victorious, come to you, bearing the voice of the Irish.' And I opened the letter with a flourish, poring over the words and hearing a loud cry from the woods of Ireland as if a great throng bore one voice. And there came to me, over and over again, the words, 'We appeal to you, holy servant boy, to come and walk among us.'"

"They knew you were a servant?"

"I cannot explain how they knew, but in that moment I was convinced to return to Ireland bearing the Gospel of the Lord Jesus to penetrate the deep darkness that enshrouds this land. To be a bringer of the forgiveness and grace of Christ and to herald the mercy of the Cross! And if I am to be an ambassador of His grace, there is one I must extend grace to first. My former master, Oengus."

"We are returning to your master?" Drustan was incredulous. "Are you attempting to get captured again?"

"I make no such attempt, good Drustan," Patrick calmly replied. "If God has truly called me to return, He will prepare me for every threat. We are not told to live or die. Our orders are to go. Come, for the hills are easy toward the coast, but they will become more difficult on the road to Oengus' house."

Brother Patrick was not joking about these hills, thought Drustan as they scaled the most recent one that gave a good view of rolling green fields. Leaning on his walking stick, Drustan called out, "Which direction from here? We've been walking for days and darkness will soon be upon us this evening."

Patrick looked around and pointed northwest. "That gnarled oak atop the hill of standing stones lies half a mile from Oengus' villa. We will be able to see him from there and then I can approach him for reconciliation."

The two men labored to descend the first hill and ascend the next one, but when they finally reached the oak, it was to behold a scene neither could believe!

"That fire!" Drustan cried, pointing in the distance. "Is that your master's house?"

Patrick could not believe what his eyes saw. The beautiful villa, the source of so many memories and much hardship, was engulfed in searing flames, and black smoke billowed from the crumbling frame to the heavens. Throughout the villa grounds, frightened horses, cattle, and sheep scattered about into the fields for a measure of safety.

Drustan stood at Patrick's side. "Sire, I do not understand? The fire looks freshly started. It can't have been burning more than twenty minutes! Can we descend the hill and see if we might find Oengus wandering about with the flocks?"

"I don't...I don't understand it," Patrick said, his lips trembling and a tear forming in the corner of his right eye, staring at the house from afar as the sun set behind it. "Oengus. Oh, Oengus, please do not be within your house at this time."

So riveted were Patrick and Drustan upon the burning house that at first they did not hear the shrieks of terror from below, nor notice the armed men scaling the hill with rage in their eyes. Finally, Drustan's ears picked up a cry from below.

"Ho, you up there! Show yourselves! There are more of us than there are of you!"

Patrick and Drustan turned around, as fifteen men, some clad in white robes and some bearing swords, swarmed over the high point of the hill, surrounding the two visitors. Patrick nodded to Drustan, who dropped his walking stick, and they both raised their hands to show themselves unarmed.

Patrick laid a comforting hand on Drustan's arm. "Druids," he whispered. "Priests and chieftains." He pointed to the thin gold bands around their necks. "I remember the gold circlets."

"Putrid travelers!" One man bellowed. "They have no native look about them! Kneel, unwelcome rogues. What brings you to these standing stones here!" He pointed his sword at Patrick, who dropped to the ground with Drustan.

"We are travelers from Britannia, both from the north of that country," cried Patrick, "and we have returned so that I might speak to the people of this island and answer their call for help."

The sword-drawn man roared, turning to three men in shining white cloaks. "Do you hear that, Cothben? Apparently, we need some kind of help! How does this feeble commoner know that?"

"I am no commoner," said Patrick, looking straight ahead toward the burning villa in the distance but keeping his voice firm. "I was the receiver of a vision from God Almighty, King of heaven and earth, in which the people of this land begged for my return to lead them from the darkness."

Almighty God, thought Drustan, that will be the death of us now with these ruffians.

The leader flashed his sword an inch from Patrick's throat. "Your return? To help us?" He gripped the hilt of his sword ferociously and narrowed his eyes. "What is your name, stranger?"

Patrick bowed his head. "My name is Patrick of Luguvalium in Britannia. Son of Calpurnius the decurion, grandson of Potitus, priest of Christ Most High. Taken by pirates to this land, where I served my master faithfully for six years. These intervening years, I have been a free man serving the Lord Jesus on my own shores until the vision that called me back here today. And for that purpose I come, to make peace between Christ and the people of this land, and first to make peace with my master." He paused, the tear coursing down his cheek. "Which looks as if I am too late."

One of the white-cloaked men approached, the one called Cothben, pointing to the flames. "Your master? Was Oengus your master?"

Patrick nodded.

Rage filled the man's face, and he shook from head to toe. "He is the one!" he screamed, pointing at Patrick. "He is the cause of this dreadful horror!" He pointed to the burning villa. "Oengus himself received word that you had come!"

"How did that happen?" asked the genuinely befuddled Patrick.

"It matters not!" roared Cothben. "He heard that his former slave had come to bear forgiveness and reconciliation to him. He knew he had acted abominably toward you. He had heard of your arrival! He could not bear that you would never seek revenge against him. The one he treated cruelly came with such purity of heart!" Cothben practically sneered out the last four words. "So he tossed himself in the flames of his own making! You forced your master to take his life!"

Patrick and Drustan shivered, certain of impending death, when another soldier called out. "Ho, my lord! We are surrounded!"

"What?" the lead soldier cried out. "Other warriors?"

"No raiding party, my lord! Wild boars ascending the hill. Fifty to sixty by the looks of it. We are certain to perish under their attack!"

Cothben ran to the edge of the hilltop and heard the snarls. Even Patrick looked down to see the approaching horde. Cothben turned and grabbed him by the front of his cloak. "You! You have brought this on us! As high priest, I demand we place you on this stone and have your blood be the sacrifice that will protect us from this vile end!" He called to the other robed men. "Priests, prepare the rock."

Drustan shivered again, this time from fear, but in that moment he saw an even more fiery color enter Patrick's eyes than from the villa below.

"Take your hands from me!" Patrick roared, shoving the high priest aside. "There will be no human sacrifice here to appease the vapors that your gods have always been! What will happen if you kill me and the boars swallow you alive? Will you go to your own death wondering why your own gods sleep?"

"You pig!" yelled another priest.

"Pig I may be, but I am a swine that serves a living God and not your false gods Dagda or Lug." Patrick walked to the cusp of the hill and raised his hands into the gathering gloom. "All who stand with me here, listen to me. I pray to the Lord of heaven, standing here with those who serve the unclean but whom shall one day be called the children of God! Christ, protect us this hour against these boars and their death-wounds, that we may receive your abundant reward of grace and mercy! Christ be with us, Christ before us, Christ behind us, Christ within us, Christ beneath us, Christ above us, Christ to our right, Christ to our left, Christ in the heart of everyone who thinks of us, Christ in the mouth of everyone who speaks to us, Christ in every eye that sees us, Christ in every ear that hears us. I bind to us now the glory and protection of the resurrected Christ the Lord!"

For a full minute, the entire party of soldiers and priests stood absolutely still. So transfixed had they been by Patrick's prayer they had forgotten their certain death at the mouths of the wild boars, until Cothben turned to the lead soldier and asked, "Faelan? Why do we not hear the boars?"

Faelan looked down, his jaw dropping in amazement. "They've gone!" He looked around the plain below. "Vanished. Without a trace!" He turned to Patrick and dropped to his knees before him. "Good man, whatever have you done to save us? If ever we doubted your intentions before and your place here, let those misgivings disappear forever! In whose name did you secure our safety?"

Patrick stepped in front of the kneeling Faelan and placed his hands on his head. "In the name of Christ, I come. In the power of Christ, you have been delivered." And he looked at Cothben. "And by the grace of Christ, this land will be washed clean."

Much of **PATRICK'S** life is clouded with mystery, with fragments from his *Confessions* and other records. Enslaved after taken by Irish pirates, Patrick escaped back to Britain where his newly-found faith gained strength and vitality as he established churches, schools, and monasteries there. His vision to return to Ireland compelled him to seek the entire island for Christ, incidentally as a prophecy circulated amongst the Druid priests and chieftains spoke of a cloaked visitor to come whom the Irish people would follow. This prophecy might have overwhelmed his former master, who chose death rather than receive the grace Patrick offered. Patrick ministered throughout Ireland, the Gospel of Christ shown compellingly through his directness of speech and his sweetness of character. He died in the mid-fifth century AD, on March 17th, which we commemorate as St. Patrick's Day today.

WHERE WE GET OUR INFORMATION

The Holy Bible, English Standard Version. John 18 & 20. Acts 1-2 & 16

Arnold, Brian. *Cyprian of Carthage: His Life and Impact.* Ross-shire, UK: Christian Focus Publications, 2017.

Augustine, *The Confessions of St. Augustine.* Translated by Albert Cook Outler. Mineola, NY: Dover Publications, 2002.

Barnes, Peter. *Athanasius of Alexandria: His Life and Impact.* Ross-shire, UK: Christian Focus Publications, 2019.

Brown, Harold O.J. *Heresies: Heresy and Orthodoxy in the History of the Church.* Peabody, MA: Hendrickson Publishers, 1998.

Casiday, Augustine and Frederick W. Norris, eds. *The Cambridge History of Christianity, Volume 2: Constantine to 600. Cambridge*, UK: Cambridge University Press, 2007.

Cyprian, *The Unity of the Church.* Ed., Dan Graves. At christianhistoryinstitute.org/study/era/module/cyprian.

Eusebius Pamphilus, *The Life of the Blessed Emperor Constantine.* Ed. Stephen Tomkins. At christianhistoryinstitute.org/study/module/constantine.

Gonzalez, Justo L. *The Story of Christianity, Volume 1: The Early Church to the Dawn of the Reformation.* New York, NY: Harper & Row, 1984.

Haykin, Michael A.G. *Patrick of Ireland: His Life and Impact.* Ross-shire, UK: Christian Focus Publications, 2017.

Holland, Tom. *Dominion: How the Christian Revolution Remade the World.* New York, NY: Basic Books, 2019.

Holmes, Michael W., ed. *The Apostolic Fathers,* Second Edition. Translated by J.B. Lightfoot and J.R. Harmer. Grand Rapids, MI: Baker Books, 1989.

Kelly, J.N.D. *Early Christian Doctrines,* rev. ed. Peabody, MA: Prince Press, 2003.

Leo I, *Sermon III: On the Third Anniversary of His Elevation to the Pontificate.* At christianhistoryinstitute.org/study/module/leo

McGrath, Alister, ed. *The Christian Theology Reader,* Third Edition. Hoboken, NJ: Wiley-Blackwell, 2006.

Mitchell, Margaret M. and Frances M. Young, eds. *The Cambridge History of Christianity, Volume 1: Origins to Constantine.* Cambridge, UK: Cambridge University Press, 2006.

Needham, Nick, ed. *Daily Readings: The Early Church Fathers.* Ross-shire, UK: Christian Heritage, 2017.

Needham, Nick. *2000 Years of Christ's Power: Volume 1: The Age of the Early Church Fathers.* Ross-shire, UK: Christian Focus Publications, 2016.

Noll, Mark. *Turning Points: Decisive Moments in the History of Christianity.* Grand Rapids, MI: Baker Academic, 2001.

Oden, Thomas C. *The Justification Reader.* Grand Rapids, MI: Eerdmans, 2002.

Olson, Roger. *The Story of Christian Theology: Twenty Centuries of Tradition and Reform.* Downers Grove, IL: IVP Academic, 1999.

Pliny the Younger, *Letter to Trajan.* Ed., Dan Graves. At christianhistoryinstitute.org/study/module/pliny.

Shelley, Bruce. *Church History in Plain Language.* Nashville, TN: Thomas Nelson, 1995.

Tertullian, *Defense.* Translated by Rev. S. Thelwall. Modernized and abridged by Stephen Tomkins. At christianhistoryinstitute.org/study/module/ tertullian.

Walton, Robert C. *Chronological and Background Charts of Church History.* Grand Rapids, MI: Zondervan, 1986.

Woodbridge, John D., ed. *Great Leaders of the Christian Church.* Chicago, IL: Moody Press, 1988.

RISEN HOPE
REIGN
THE CHURCH IN THE MIDDLE AGES
LUKE H. DAVIS

Reign

The Church in the Middle Ages

Luke H. Davis

During the Middle Ages the church labored to build a community of faith. Benedict, Columba, and Francis organized communities in which the Gospel could be preached. Theodulf, Anselm, and Bernard of Clairvaux answered the call to reform that community and theology. And when the church's leaders drifted from the authority of Scripture, a first wave of reformers in Peter Waldo, John Wycliffe, and John Hus arose to call God's people back to the grace of God.

This was a Church that sought to reign, love and conquest, a Church that wanted to secure freedom, and proclaim the gospel. When that Church fell into corruption it undertook its own reform. Which one of these is the medieval Church? They all are! And in that we can find hope in the God Who loves His Church as we seek to live in His name.

Luke Davis has written a grand "human" introduction to the Church in the Middle Ages. Focusing on the Western Church, although not ignoring the East, he enables us to encounter many of the leading Christians of the day – Churchmen, dissenters, men, women, theologians, preachers, and mystics. An ideal springboard to propel readers into further study of a sadly neglected period in church history.

Nick Needham,
Lecturer in Church History,
Highland Theological College, Dingwall, Scotland

ISBN: 978-1-5271-0801-1

John Chrysostom

The Preacher in the Emperor's Court

Dayspring Macleod

There was something about John Chrysostom and the words he spoke that lit up his world. He was an important leader of the early church, known so much for his preaching and public speaking that he was given the nickname Golden Mouth.

"It is madness to fill your cupboards with clothing while other human beings stand naked and trembling with the cold so that they can hardly hold themselves upright."

It didn't matter if you were rich or poor John spoke the truth – emphatically. Even the empress fell under his criticism which eventually led to his exile and death.

ISBN: 978-1-5271-03085

Augustine
The Truth Seeker
K. C. Murdarasi

Although his mother was a faithful Christian, Augustine managed to stray into a sinful life. His life changed when he realised the truth of the Gospel. Augustine became a bishop and a tower of faith in the early church. His life is a glimpse into the days of Roman Africa and a powerful picture of the wisdom and durability of God's Word in a pagan culture.

ISBN: 978-1-78191-296-6

Christian Focus Publications publishes books for adults and children under its four main imprints: Christian Focus, CF4K, Mentor and Christian Heritage. Our books reflect our conviction that God's Word is reliable and Jesus is the way to know him, and live for ever with him.

Our children's publication list covers pre-school to early teens. We also publish personal and family devotional titles, biographies and inspirational stories that children will love.

From pre-school board books to teenage apologetics, we have it covered!

Christian Focus Publications Ltd,
Geanies House, Fearn, Ross-shire,
IV20 1TW, Scotland,
United Kingdom.

Find us at our web page:
www.christianfocus.com